MAX POWER

TOP MAD MOTORS, TOP TOTTY, TOP ICE, TOP CRUISES, TOP SPEED, TOP BOOK

Compiled by Paul Donnelley

CHAMELEON

MEAN, MODIFIED AND STREET-LEGAL

Compiled by Paul Donnelley

CHAMELEON

First published in Great Britain in 1998 by Chameleon Books
an imprint of André Deutsch Ltd
76 Dean Street
London W1V 5HA

André Deutsch Ltd is a VCI plc company

www.vci.co.uk

Printed by Butler and Tanner, Somerset and London

A catalogue record for this book is available from the British Library

ISBN 0 233 99582 X

contents

Classic Cars 7

Top Totty 87

ICE is Nice 99

Cruisin' 125

The Max Power Crew 133

The Jokes 140

CHAPTER 1
CLASSIC CARS

To kick off we are taking a look at ten –
count 'em – ten, of the classiest,
sassiest cars to hit the road over the
past twelve months or so. Just sit back
and feast your minces on these beauties
as all your birthdays come at once!

Astra-nutt

ASTRA GSI

THE FIRST TIME is always a momentous one in anyone's life. First snog, first shag, but much more importantly, first car. Marcus Thomas was no different when he splurged a serious five figure sum on this Astra GSi.

When Marcus first laid eyes on the Twin-DTM exhaust, Renault 19 roof spoiler and 17" (40.8cm) Venoms...he was in absolute fucking heaven.

The immaculate job on the bodywork had been performed by Peter and James at Manic Motorsport, two dedicated chaps as ever we came across. They happily spent their evenings modifying roof spoilers, fibre-glassing bumpers and the like. On the subject of fibreglassing bumpers, Peter and James came up with a spiffing idea – replace the existing one with a bumper from an Escort Cosworth. Trouble was, it was too wide, so our dynamic duo cut it in half and then fibreglassed it together again. Simple when you know how!

Next up they put Espace and Impreza vents on the bonnet and finished off the front with twin headlights from Steinmetz. They also thoughtfully came up with the

Astra-nut

mirrors and skirts. Under those vents there is an enormous 315bhp. The 2.0-litre, 16-valve engine has been tuned to the max. The bottom end's been lightened and balanced, high torque cams have been added and a new Courtenay engine management system has been put in place to run the show. Cooling mods to the block and head mean that there's a better water flow to the head, and the main power thrust is created by a Garrett T28 hybrid turbo.

Stopping is no problem either. The car has cross-drilled and grooved Brembo blanks at the front and 12-grooved Brembo blanks at the back. Chassis Dynamics springs and Koni shocks have upgraded the Astra's normal suspension into a more substantial arrangement.

A strange touch this – the driver's door handle came from a Vectra, but the passenger side door doesn't have a handle at all. The rear has been finished off with a turbo badge from a Cavalier and metallic grey boot trim. Other finishing touches worth a mention include a single wiper that does a full sweep and oval repeaters sprayed red. All in all, it's one mutha of a car.

Astra-nut

Astra-nut

Max Fax

ENGINE: 2-litre, 4-cylinder, 16-valve with Garrett T28 hybrid turbo; low compression pistons, bottom end lightened and balanced, cooling modifications to block and head, breather modifications in head and cam cover, high-torque cams, new cast manifold, Courtenay engine management system, Calibra Turbo radiator with intercooler on side, charge cooler; Courtenay exhaust system with twin 7.2cm (2.8") Scorpion tailpipes.

TRANSMISSION: Factory 5-speed manual gearbox.

SUSPENSION: Chassis Dynamics springs and Koni shocks front and back; lowered 3cm (1.2") all round.

BRAKES: Front – cross-drilled and grooved Brembo blanks, standard calipers and uprated Vauxhall pads; back – 12-grooved Brembo blanks, standard calipers and uprated Vauxhall pads.

WHEELS AND TYRES: 7"x17" (17.8cmx43.2cm) TSW Venoms with Goodyear Eagle 215/40 ZR17 rubber.

BODYWORK: Escort Cosworth front bumper modified to fit, Subaru Impreza bonnet vents, Renault Espace vent on front right wing, Steinmetz twin headlamps and grille, wing mirrors and side skirts, oval side repeaters sprayed red, single wiper conversion, Renault 19 16v rear roof spoiler, later spec metallic grey boot trim, turbo badge from a Cavalier, Regal filler cap; complete respray in Flame Red.

INTERIOR: Red dials and leather gear gaiter.

ICE: Sony CD head unit and 10-disc changer, 2x Panasonic 6x9s on rear parcel shelf, Soundlab amp, 2x 10" (25.4cm) subs in the boot.

The Sky's the limit

666 BAD

NISSAN SKYLINE R33 GT-R

The

Sky's the limit

THE PLATE ON THIS CAR says it all: 666 BAD. What it should read is SATAN'S VERY OWN JALOPY FROM THE SEVENTH PLANE OF SITH but there isn't room for that. Suffice to say, this Skyline GTR is absurdly good. So much so that it should be dubbed the greatest car in this book (apart from the 1000bhp Japan-based Skyline you'll see later).

What has it got? Best to ask what hasn't it got. This R33 has more gadgets than an Inspector Gadget Fan Club World Conference, and that's a lot. Not only does it have intelligent four wheel drive, which dishes out torque to the front wheels when you really need it, it has something called Super Hicas Four Wheel Steering, which turns the front and rear wheels in opposite directions when you're sideways, and active suspension to keep things on the level. Add to that a fantastic Brembo antilock braking system and you have a performance package that'll leave almost any supercar behind in any weather.

The engine? One of the best in the world, Nissan's rock solid 2.6-litre straight six. But of course, it's not standard here, oh no. Two (please count them, 2) gigantic HKS blowers help fan the fires in this thing's satanic core, blowing it to 450 horses. It whines and chuffs and wheezes, and best of all it revs, all the way to the 8000rpm limiter. With two extra cylinders and an extra turbo, not to mention all the clever suspension and drivetrain bits, this car, to put it bluntly, pisses on any Cosworth.

The Skyline looks as tough as any car, too. Many Max readers don't appreciate the GTR's looks, but this writer thinks they're just about perfect: it's a proper three box car shape, long nose, engine up front where it should be, aggressive nose and headlights, big, big 18in Nismo wheels beneath flared arches. It's perfect. And it has a boot. Crave a GTR badly. It's the best car on the planet.

The Sky's the limit

The Sky's the limit

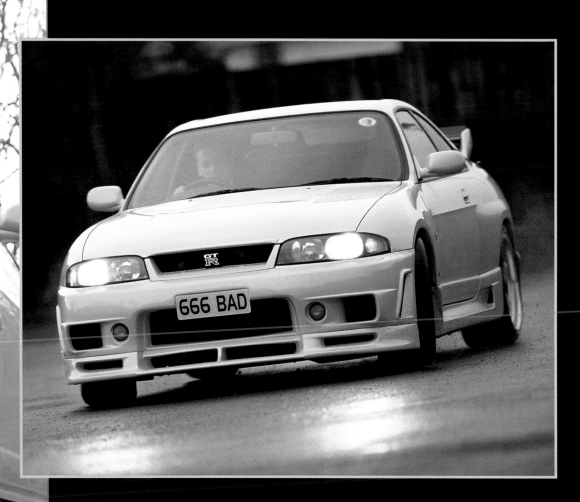

666 BAD

Max Fax

ENGINE: 2568cc, twin-cam straight six, 24-valve; variable valve timing, iron block, alloy head, twin-ceramic modified HKS turbos, HKS power flow twin-air intakes (one for each turbo); uprated and reprogrammed management system; HKS Super Dragger stainless steel exhaust system with 12cm (4.7") tailpipe.

TRANSMISSION: 5-speed, close ratio gearbox, Attesa computer-controlled, four-wheel drive.

SUSPENSION: Fully independent. Active multi-link with uprated anti-roll bars; springs and dampers all round; adjustable front and rear anti-roll bars and Super Hicas four-wheel steering.

BRAKES: Brembo discs and callipers all round; standard ABS.

WHEELS & TYRES: Front – 9"x18" (22.8cmx45.7cm) Nismo 3-piece alloys with 265/35 18 Continental Conti-Sport Contact rubber; rear – 10"x18" (25.4x45.7cm) Nismo 3-piece alloys with 285/35 18 Continental Conti-Sport Contact rubber.

BODYWORK: Aluminium body, Nismo bodykit comprising 3-piece front bumper, side skirts and carbon fibre rear fin; painted pearl yellow.

INTERIOR: As standard.

PERFORMANCE: Max power – 450bhp; Max speed: 170mph; 0-60mph in 3.8 seconds.

Top Hamann!!

BMW COMPACT M3

LAST TIME I LOOKED, a BMW M3 coupe weighed precisely 1471kgs. Now, before you run off shouting 'irrelevant and unimportant', you should know that the Hamann M3 Compact you see on these pages has had a full 300kgs knocked out of the standard M3's mass. Yes, 300 kay-gees, gone. Not there. Vapourised. Kaput.

This operation, by my maths, will see the Hamann weighing in at a spritely 1171kgs, or thereabouts. That's only a bee's dick more than a boggo 1.8 Ford Escort, and somewhat less than a Toyota Corolla or a two-litre Peugeot 306.

Now, add the glorious M3 straight six engine to this lightweight body and tune it a bit - new filter, exhaust, chip, let it pump out 352bhp rather than the puny 321bhp of the standard car. The result is what they call, in the trade, a healthy power to weight ratio.

This car has had almost every bit of interior removed. It's shed more kit than Demi Moore. Forget the door trims and window winders, they're replaced by thin pieces of carbon fibre and a couple of bits of wire to release the doors. The windows are up and that's where they stay. There is no airconditioning, no carpet or soundproofing material, no rear seats. Just a roll cage to help stiffen the handling and make it even more racer-like, and a couple of super-light Recaro A8 racing buckets. As well as a steering wheel and gearlever and some drilled alloy pedals so you can drive the thing. Check out the wing mirrors: they're lightweight STW jobs. Nice.

Let's get back to the power to weight equation: this car only lugs around 3.32 kilos for every horsepower it develops. That's less than a Ferrari F355 (3.74), less than a Lamborghini Diablo VT (3.37), and less than a Dodge Viper (3.805). So, to coin another technical term, it goes quite well (as a quick reference, the world's fastest road car, the McLaren F1, only carries 1.81 kilos per brake horsepower and a Formula One Car carries 759 grams. Oh well, there's always someone with better kit).

This Beemer has the full monty with wheels, 18in HM2s, and the car sits low and squat on Hamann suspension. The bodykit is aerodynamically sculpted to help stick the car to the road at speed.

And the price? Don't ask.

Top Hamann!!

Top Hamann!!

Max Fax

ENGINE: 3200cc, 6-cylinder, 24-valve; Hamann airbox, re-mapped ECU; full stainless steel exhaust system with twin-DTM 7.2cm (3") tailpipes.

TRANSMISSION: M3 6-speed manual gearbox.

SUSPENSION: Hamann springs front and rear, lowered 2" (5cm) all round; front – Hamann shocks; rear – GFX shocks.

BRAKES: Standard E36 M3 spec front and rear.

WHEELS & TYRES: Front – Hamann 'Peachy' 9"x18" (22.8cmx45.7cm) 3-piece split-rims with 6cm (2.4") offset and 235/40 ZR18 Yokohama A-008P tyres; rear – Hamann 'Peachy' 12"x18" (30.5cmx45.7cm) 3-piece split-rims with 6cm (2.4") offset and 285/35 ZR18 Yokohama A-008P tyres.

BODYWORK/PAINT: Full list of Hamann STW parts including front and rear bumpers, two front splitters, side skirts, front and rear wings, rear spoiler and indicators, M3 wing mirrors, tinted rear windows; respray in black.

INTERIOR: Recaro A8 racing seats, Schroth 3-point harnesses, Momo steering wheel, carbon fibre effect gearknob, carbon fibre effect dial kit, real carbon fibre detailing on door panels and around gearknob area.

ICE: Clarion ARX-917OR head unit, Clarion CDC-605 6-disc changer, 2x Kenwood tweeters, 4x Focal tweeters (two on the parcel shelf), 4x Focal 6x9s (two on the parcel shelf), 2x Focal F180X crossovers, Sony XM-10020 2-channel amp, 2x Audio Mobile Acoustic 12" (30.5cm) 400W subs.

PERFORMANCE: Max power – 352bhp; max speed – 172mph; 0-60mph – 5.1 seconds.

Get outta my dreams, get into my

KA

LS DESIGN'S FORD KA

Get outta my dreams, get into my KA

SILLY NAME ASIDE, Ford's Ka is an interesting Ka. I mean car. (If you want to read it the same way I'm writing it, please pronounce 'Ka' as 'cat' without the 't').

Whatever you might think of the standard cat-without-the-'t', you have to admit that Austrian firm MS Design has done a good job here. One of the biggest styling problems on the boggo car are the grey wheel arches and bumpers, which attract too much attention as cheap plasticky oval curvy bits breaking up the clean general shape. It makes the Ka look dumpy and toyish and half-finished and stupid (if you've ever seen a Ka with the wheel arches painted the same colour as the body, you'll notice the improvement instantly). MS identified this problem and fixed it, with excellent new front and rear bumpers that draw your eye to body colour lower down, helping to lower the car visually and using the grey bits to break up the shape. The low sideskirts help too, along with the trick lowering suspension which drops the car 30mm.

Add a proper set of arch-filling MS wheels (only 15 inches in diameter, though they look bigger) and we have a Ka which is squat and tough and won't be shamed by any small fast Ford. Replace the awful little 8V 1.3 four with a Puma 1.8 16V, change the name and the job's done. A car with Ka-racter.

Get outta my dreams, get into my

Get outta my dreams, get into my

Max Fax

ENGINE: 1299cc, 4-cylinder, 8-valve fuel-injected; MS Design back box.

TRANSMISSION: Factory 5-speed manual gearbox.

SUSPENSION: MS Design lowering springs front and back, lowered 3cm (1.2") all round.

BRAKES: Front – factory discs; back – factory drums.

WHEELS AND TYRES: 7"x15" (17.8cmx38cm) Topline MS10 wheels with 195/45 R15 Pirelli P700-Z rubber.

BODYWORK/PAINT: MS Design bodykit consisting of front bumper and grille, side skirts, back bumper and back roof spoiler with brake light.

INTERIOR: Complete blue leather with red piping on seats and steering wheel, painted dashboard and colour-coded centre console; gearknob and gaiter trimmed in leather.

ICE: Standard radio cassette.

SECURITY: Alarm and immobiliser.

PERFORMANCE: Max power – 60bhp; Max speed – 96mph; 0-60mph – 14.3 seconds.

A VERY SPESH
FORD ESCORT

Let's all meet in project 2000

Let's all meet in project 2000

MAX POWER PROJECT CARS just get better and better and better. First there was RS Kicker, which did just that: kicked RS. Then there was XS, a purple wide-arched BMW 3-series which was XS-ive in the extreme. Thunder, perhaps the most popular of all, was a Vauxhall Carlton with a Courtenay Turbo-ed engine, two rear wings and a stereo system loud enough generate its own weather system. Then came Project 2000, surely the greatest Max car yet.

I'll never forget the moment I first saw Project 2000. I was dawdling round one of the many large roundabouts in Max Power's hideously dull home town of Peterborough, minding my own business in a V6 Mondeo. Suddenly my ears were assaulted by an engine note loud enough to shatter the silence in my cosy little cocoon, the sort of sound that immediately pricks your brain to find its source. It was massively, insanely loud.

There it was! A fleeting shape in my mirror, a bright pink Escort going at tremendous speed, taking the first exit, the one I'd just passed. It had emerged from the slip road and shot left, howling probably the best engine note I've heard on any road car. The driver was Gez Jones, grinning. I was going straight on, but decided to fly around the roundabout and give chase. The Mondeo's tyres howled: I knew I'd have to get my foot down to get anywhere near him.

By the time I'd reached the exit Project 2000 had taken, and shot onto the road doing over 100mph. It was gone. Disappeared. I reached 130mph giving chase, but Gez was long gone. Only he would be able to tell us how fast he was going down that dual carriageway. Maybe he'd prefer not to say.

If there is a point to my little story, it's this: Project 2000 means nothing until you see it and hear it at speed. Read the spec for all the details, wonder at the ICE and the paintwork, but know that the Mountune engine is a jewel, a work of art, and its bellow is glorious enough to make your head fall off with wonder.

Let's all meet in project 2000

2000

Let's all meet in project

Max Fax

ENGINE: 1998cc, 16-valve; 4-cylinder, Mountune air filter, aluminium inlet trumpets, Mountune throttle bodies, Weber injections manufactured to Mountune's specific flow rates, slide throttle linkage, inlet and exhaust port sizes increased and hand finished, Group 'A' lightened and shaped inlet valves, shaped exhaust valves, machined cam followers, solid lifters, heavy duty single valve springs, Kent cams to Mountune secret specification, grooved and ringed engine block, Group 'A' cylinder head gasket. Mountune forged pistons with machined pockets, Mountune forged con rods, balanced production crank, Mountune crank positioning sensor (uprated on standard Ford item), Ford EC4 engine management system with Mountune input module, a bit of stainless steel overbraiding hosing here and there, Fram oil filter, Repsol synthetic race oil; Magnex 5.4cm (2") stainless steel exhaust with double pass back box and twin DTM centre-exit tailpipes.

TRANSMISSION: 5-speed manual RS2000 gearbox with minimal tolerance gear clusters, polished internals, Mountune motorsport F2 clutch, Repsol synthetic oils.

SUSPENSION: The massive roll-cage stiffens the chassis, so strut braces aren't needed; Spax 'RSX Race' dampers with height-adjustable platforms and 5.4cm (2") springs all round, bump and rebound adjustment at rear.

BRAKES: Full Escort Cosworth brake system fitted by Gordon Spooner Engineering, steel braided brake hosing, DOT 5.1 fluid; front – Escort Cosworth calipers and Black Diamond grooved and drilled discs with Predator fast-road pads; back – Escort Cosworth calipers and Black Diamond grooved and drilled discs with Predator fast-road pads.

WHEELS AND TYRES: TSW Imola 7"x17" (17.7cmx43cm) alloy wheels (Escort Cosworth offset) complete with all the alloy gubbins you can handle, 235/40 17i Yokohama AVS (AV1-40i) tyres.

BODYWORK/PAINT: Standard rally spec RS2000 arches, modified sills, modified Escort Cosworth WRC rear spoiler. Morette twin-headlight conversion, reshaped standard RS2000 front bumper/spoiler, reshaped standard back bumper with ally exhaust heat shield, filled sunroof, Ghia grille surround, rally spec roof scoop and bonnet grille, carbon fibre DTM-style door mirrors, debadged boot, recessed side repeaters, locks off, painted in Porsche Karmin Rot.

INTERIOR: 14-point FIA spec roll-cage providing fantastic structural rigidity and painted in lime green; lots of carpeting, remanufactured door panels and retrimmed by Huets, two ex-works FIA-approved Ford rally seats, Schroth 5-point harnesses, Momo steering wheel with Snap-Off boss, Raid gearknob.

ICE spec

SOUND SOURCE: Denon DCT-1000 head unit.

AMPLIFICATION: 1x Infinity Beta BD-50 (2x 50W amp), 2x Infinity Beta BD-100 (2x 100W amp), 1x Infinity Beta BD-300 (2x 300W amp).

PROCESSORS: Infinity 2XE active crossover, various crossovers supplied with the UniPlane 62F speakers.

SPEAKERS: Front doors – 2x UniPlane 62F speakers 6" (15.2cm); floor-mounted – 2x UniPlane 80F 8" (20.3cm); rear fill – 2x UniPlane 62F speakers 6" (15.2cm); subs – 4x Beta 12 12" (30.5cm) boxed subs.

CABLES: Phoenix Gold Pro and Expert cables used throughout, special screws and better designed block.

POWER SUPPLY: Escort diesel alternator, uprated Optima battery.

NICE INSTALL BITS: Cables thro' stainless steel overbraid.

Turbo power

MAX

WEST MIDLANDS RS CENTRE
Tel: 01902 403303

RS TURBO SERIES 2

THE NISSAN SKYLINE GTR is an exotic, a supercar, but some would say it means nothing to the average Max Power reader, and is therefore a waste of time. Much more noble to modify a car we can all relate to, make a monster out of a bread-and-butter machine, to terrorise other motorists with something they can only just barely recognise. Such is John Lawman's amazing RS Turbo, probably the best ever seen in Max Power. And there've been a few RS Turbos in Max over the years. Let's look at the engine first. It pumps out 325bhp, quite a lot for an RS Turbo. In fact, it's a stonking amount of power. The turbo itself is a Turbo Dynamics item, with the standard 270 degree thrust bearing replaced with a more supportive 360 degree item. It also supports a bigger compressor wheel, a larger compressor cover and an uprate actuator. Doing all this work to the turbo alone gives you an idea of how serious this car is.

John knew that 1.9 litre conversions to the RS Turbo's standard 1.6 have been around for a while, so he stripped it and tried an experiment.

'It's actually a 2.2 litre engine now,' he says. 'The only problem is that it's a bit lairy'.

The head is the only part left from the original engine. It's been heavily modified, but it's still the original. It's been flowed and had an enlarged inlet and exhaust valves squeezed in. To keep the valves opening and shutting nicely, a Piper 285-T2 cam has been installed.

A Zetec bottom end has been slapped in place using Mahle over-sized forged pistons and total seal piston rings. There are other bits from Cosworth in here, which help the engine rev higher. Basically, this engine is hotter than the hottest chilli dish in the world's hottest curry house, on a hot day.

The bodykit is a Kerscher wide arch. Funny how fashion changes. At one stage, wide bodies were out, but with the advent of wide-arch kit cars on the world rally scene, they're back in. This kit suits the Scort perfectly, just subtle enough not to ruin the basic shape, and the 15 coats of paint used here give it a lustre unseen on any previous Max power feature car. The best Escort on earth? Absolutely.

Turbo power

Max Fax

ENGINE: 2198cc, 8-valve; 4-cylinder, fuel-injected, turbocharged; flowed cylinder head, machined and wire-ringed block, Piper 285-T2 cam, enlarged inlet and exhaust valves, inlet and exhaust ports matched to manifolds, Zetec 2-litre pistons and con rods, balanced 1.8-litre crankshaft, 1.8-litre oil pump, dump valve with kevlar diaphragm, fifth injector controlled by Superchips Icon-X system, Turbo Dynamics hybrid turbo, Pipercross air filter with alloy bonnet vent cover; Scorpion 6cm (2.4") stainless steel exhaust with 10.8cm (4.25") tailpipe.

TRANSMISSION: 5-speed diesel gearbox with Zetec clutch.

SUSPENSION: Koni adjustable dampers with 30mm lowering springs all round.

BRAKES: Front – factory discs, Mintex 1144 brake pads; back – Sierra 4x4 rear disc conversion utilising modified Escort handbrake cable with standard discs, Mintex 1144 pads.

WHEELS AND TYRES: Image split-rim five-spoke alloys; front – 9"x17" (22.8cmx43.2cm) wheels with 235/40 17 Toyo Proxes T1 tyres; back – 10"x17" (25.4cmx43.2cm) wheels with 265/40 17 Toyo Proxes T1 tyres.

BODYWORK/PAINT: Kerscher wide-arch bodykit, Morette twin-headlamp conversion, fabricated stainless steel bonnet vents, flush-fit alloy filter flaps, coated in Radiant Red (applied using two coats of filler primer, nine coats of primer and three coats of red).

INTERIOR: RS Turbo seats retrimmed in black leather with red piping; Raid red steering wheel and matching gearknob; Snap-Off steering wheel boss.

ICE: Binatone head unit with two Audioline speakers.

SECURITY: As if we'd divulge!!

PERFORMANCE: Max power – 325bhp; 0-60mph – 'about 6 seconds'.

Turbo

HONDA CRX

YO MAX

CRX-Y

EVER SEEN A WILDER CAR in your whole goddamn worthless miserable honky life? No? Of course you haven't. Never, ever, has there been a wilder car to grace the pages of Max Power. Faster, yes, more tasteful, perhaps, but wilder? Never. I guess it's appropriate that it should come from the world's greatest and most powerful nation. And the one with the biggest drug problem.

Contrary to what you might think, the guy driving the Honda CRX in these shots, Shaun Carlson, isn't the owner. That lucky chap, who shall remain anonymous, was too busy working trying to pay for the mods and paintwork. See, the owner had taken two extra jobs to try to help pay for the work, and was just handing his extra paycheques straight over to Shaun, who built the car. Time off wasn't an option, even for Max Power. The engine's about as spectacular as the paintwork, bodywork and interior. It's a 1.6 VTEC with a million internal upgrades and a monster Garrett T4 turbo bolted on, running 28lbs of boost, which is good for 350bhp. The short side exit exhaust is neat, and the gigantic Nitrous kit helps it run even more power: those two skull-painted bottles in the cabin equal a gallon of the good stuff, controlled by a couple of paddles on the steering wheel, and the engine itself drinks pure alcohol dragster fuel of 118 octane. With the gas at full blow, it adds up to 500bhp and gives the car 0-60mph acceleration of 3.5 seconds. There's almost nothing left of the original body, which helps performance enormously. The kit is mostly lightweight fibreglass Mugen stuff. Inside, everything is gone: just a seat, a cage, a harness, a set of lightweight Auto Meter gauges in place of the dash, and some ancillaries. The car weighs 743 kilos in total, which is nothing, cigarette packet stuff.

There's never been anything like it in Max Power before and probably nothing will ever beat it. I need to go and lie down for a minute now. Bye.

CRX-Y

CRX-Y

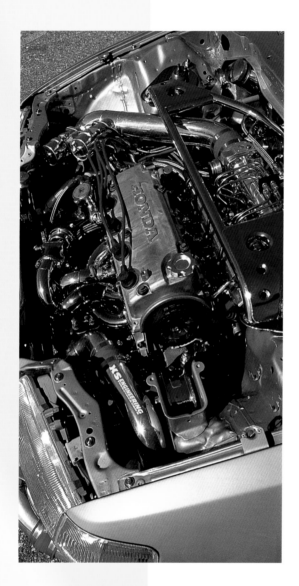

Max Fax

ENGINE:	1590cc, 4-cylinder, 16-valve with double overhead cam; 1.6 V-tec head; uprated valves; springs and cams; ARP head studs, Felpro head gasket, NuFormz blockguard, JE 8.5-1 compression pistons, chrome Cunningham rods, balanced blueprinted and polished crank; NuFormz stainless steel exhaust manifold, XS Engineering hybrid Garrett T4 turbo with ceramic coated turbine housing, Richard Lee Wastegate, XL DF1 fuel injection unit, 4x RC Engineering 720cc injectors, RC Engineering throttle body, 2x Greddy blow-off valves, Paxton fuel pump and regulator; G&J Aircraft stainless steel lines, hoses and fittings; car running on 118 octane VP gasoline; full NuFormz exhaust system with 7.2cm (3") side-exit tailpipe.
TRANSMISSION:	5-speed manual gearbox, full metallic ACT clutch, welded Heli-Arc differentials, new bearings, 1.6 axles from Japanese spec Honda Integra.
SUSPENSION:	Apex 6-way adjustable shocks and Neuspeed springs all round with chrome-plated suspension components.
BRAKES:	Front – Brembo drilled discs, Performance Friction pads, chrome-plated Integra calipers; back – standard.
WHEELS AND TYRES:	7"x18" (17.8cmx45.7cm) Volk Racing Volk III wheels with Nitto NT-450 215/35 ZR18 rubber.
BODYWORK/PAINT:	Mugen fibreglass bodykit consisting of detachable front and back bumpers and side skirts, Oki fibreglass rear hatch, Tit-Crew fibreglass bonnet, gutted doors and alloy door panels, MR-5 Lexun plastic windows; green respray by NuFormz followed by Kal Koncepts graphics and airbrushing by Air Syndicates.
INTERIOR:	Momo carbon fibre race seat, Momo steering wheel with built-in nitrous switches, Simpson 5-point harnesses, interior stripped by NuFormz, Auto Meter lightweight gauges, Apex AVCR boost control, MSD 7AL-2 ignition system, 2x 10lbs nitrous bottles, rear of seat and nitrous bottles airbrushed to match exterior.
SECURITY:	It's in America.
PERFORMANCE:	Max power – 500bhp; 0-60mph – 3.5 seconds; maximum speed – 169mph.

Turning Japanese

NISSAN SKYLINE GTR
AND TOYOTA SUPRA

RUMOURS OF 1000BHP SKYLINE GTRS had been filtering into these shores for several years before Max writer Hans Seeberg went to Tokyo and actually found one. Then the rumours stopped. Now it's fact, thanks to Taka the Otter and the rest of the chaps at Top Secret Performance Engineering. As we've seen earlier in this tome, the Nissan Skyline GTRs' straight six is one of the most tunable engines in the world. Still, you might wonder how a six of only 2.7 litres could possibly develop anything near 1000 bhp. A V8 or V12 maybe, but a six? Well, there's nothing to it, really: turbocharged 1.5 litre four and six-cylinder formula one cars of the late eighties were developing over 1400bhp. Even tiny supercharged engines of the 1930s were developing 600bhp. It all comes down to the 'B' word: Boost.

A Japanese friend of mine, Mr T, who runs the Midnight Club street racing gang in Tokyo (where they see speeds of over 200mph on public roads, mostly in Skylines) has a prized possession in a glass cabinet hanging on the wall of his living room. It is a Garrett T67 turbocharger, cut away artistically to reveal its innards. It is like a shrine to the guy, because he, more than anyone, is aware of how much power two of those turbos will give him. His Skyline develops around 750bhp, enough to see over 200mph in the right conditions. I've been in the car with him at 170mph and it feels like it's just ticking over.

It is a huge unit, the T67, bigger than a small household fan. With

Turning Japanesese

Turning Japanese

two of them attached to this unburstable RB26 engine, 500bhp is possible without a major upgrade of engine internals! At 1000bhp of boost, forged pistons, titanium conrods and uprated cams, coolers, pumps and gaskets are necessary to prevent detonation. In these engines, the parts are supplied by famous Japanese Skyline tuner, Trust.

This GTR will run the standing quarter mile in 9.6 seconds, and even more impressively, will reach 200mph in just 23.99 seconds, a Japanese record. The Supra holds the 2wd record to 180mph at 24.7 seconds. You don't need to know much more about these cars, except, perhaps, what it's like to ride in them.

Over to Hans, in the GTR:

'The boost kicks in, then kicks in some more. The phenomenal acceleration intensifies with every second. Taka shouts something across but it's lost in the engine's screams. We enter a tunnel and as the lights shoot past I feel like I'm in a Millennium Falcon simulator entering hyperspace. All I can do is desperately try to tense my stomach muscles to keep my wee wee in'.

God knows, and that was only a short burst in third.

Turning Japanese

歩行者用押ボタン

Max Fax
Toyota Supra

ENGINE: 2700cc, straight-six, RB26 24-valve; HKS pistons, titanium conrods, fully-balanced crankshaft, Apex long-duration camshafts, two HKS-modified Garrett 3037 turbos, uprated fuel pumps and collector tanks, 4-row intercooler, 16-row oil cooler, custom intercooler with polished piping, Top Secret-designed Competizione Rom ECU, Top Secret muffler with full Top Secret stainless steel exhaust system and 9.6cm (4") tailpipe.

TRANSMISSION: Trust 6-speed gearbox with OS triple-plate clutch and Nismo differentials.

SUSPENSION: Öhlins height-adjustable shock absorbers with Eilbach twin springs front and rear; aluminium bushes, uprated tension rods, lowered 5cm (2") all round.

BRAKES: Front – Trust 33.6cm (13.2") discs with Alcon G-Rex pads and calipers; rear – Brembo kit consisting of 31.2cm (12.3") discs, pads and calipers.

WHEELS AND TYRES: Front – 9"x18" (22.8cmx45.7cm) Volk Racing Challenge with 255/35 ZR18 Advan Neova tyres; back – 10"x18" (25.4cmx45.7cm) Volk Racing Challenge with 275/35 ZR18 Advan Neova tyres.

BODYWORK/PAINT: Full G-Force fibreglass bodykit for downforce consisting of front and back bumpers, side skirts, rear wing and mirrors; gold respray.

INTERIOR: Recaro SP-J Raptor seats custom-covered in red, Personal Actis wheel, Stack system, boost gauge plus gauges to monitor exhaust temperature, turbo pressure, fuel and oil pressure.

ICE: CD and Mini-Disc player, TV and video, mids and 2x 10" (25.4cm) speakers.

PERFORMANCE: Max power – 1003bhp; 0-180mph – 24.7 seconds; maximum speed – 200+mph.

Max Fax
Nissan Skyline GTR

ENGINE: 2700cc, RB26 straight-six, 24-valve; Trust engine parts consisting of forged pistons, titanium conrods, fully-balanced crankshaft, long-duration camshafts, uprated gaskets, uprated oil pump, 4-row intercooler, 16-row oil cooler, two Garrett T67 turbochargers, three Bosch fuel pumps, custom intercooler with polished piping, Top Secret-designed Competizione Rom ECU, Top Secret stainless steel exhaust manifold, Top Secret muffler with full Top Secret stainless steel exhaust and 9.6cm (4") tailpipe.

TRANSMISSION: Trust 6-speed gearbox with OS triple-plate clutch and Nismo differentials.

SUSPENSION: Öhlins height-adjustable shock absorbers with Eilbach twin springs front and rear; aluminium bushes, uprated tension rods, lowered 5cm (2") all round.

BRAKES: Front – Brembo 33.6cm (13.2") vented and grooved discs, Project 'U' pads and Brembo calipers front and rear.

WHEELS AND TYRES: 9"x18" (22.8cmx45.7cm) Volk Racing TE37s with Advan Neova 265/35 ZR18 tyres.

BODYWORK/PAINT: Full G-Force fibreglass bodykit for downforce consisting of front and back bumpers, side skirts, rear wing and mirrors; gold respray.

INTERIOR: Recaro SPGN race seats, Sabelt 4-point harnesses, Stack digital dash system including boost gauge plus gauges to monitor exhaust temperature, turbo pressure, fuel and oil pressure.

PERFORMANCE: Max power – 1003bhp; 0-200mph – 23.99 seconds; quarter mile – 9.6 seconds; maximum speed – 200+mph.

Bright as a Button

DIMMA SUPERCHARGED 306 MAXI

Bright as a Button

NO LAG. That's the thing about a supercharger. It's driven by a belt directly off the engine, so the instant you hit the throttle, your boost is at hand. The effect on a motor is a thing of wonder to behold: it's as if the capacity is increased, as if angry angels are pushing. Urge is magnified everywhere.

'It's a deceptive sort of power because it's so smooth,' says Terry Pankhurst, boss of Dimma UK, supplier of this car's amazing wide-arch bodykit.

'The car's power has been uprated from 160bhp to 230, so that's a good effect straight away. But it's strange: you only tend to notice the improvement when you line up a supercharged car against a standard one: it's especially effective higher up the speed range, say between 80mph and 120mph. In this sort of situation, my car will leave the standard one way behind. And it'll pull just as well from 30mph in fifth'.

This action is accompanied by a distant whistle in the engine bay, a bit like the whine you hear when your radio speakers are picking up engine revs.

'It's actually more noticeable outside the car', reckons Terrry. It's not a particularly inspiring sound, but it gives you an idea something weird is going on, which is what you need.

The supercharger here is an Orpcon unit, priced at around four grand, fitted, including a charge cooler and chip. Terry's also fitted a Tube Torque custom exhaust to help the breathing, ending proudly in a 4in tailpipe. Nice.

Inside, the Dimma is awesome, with a full Huets ICE install. Check the spec for all the details, but it's enough to say that this is a very fine job indeed.

With that amazing bodykit, which is the same unit fitted to Peugeot's rally kit cars, and 17in Compomotive wheels, this is a Pug to die for, and no mistake.

utton

Bright as a Button

Max Fax

ENGINE: 1998cc, 16-valve; Orpcon Supercharger with exchange inlet manifold, replacement alternator, thick head gasket, charge cooler with electric water pump hoses and reservoir; 240bhp engine management chip; Tube Torque custom exhaust system with 9.6cm (3.8") tailpipe.

TRANSMISSION: Standard 5-speed manual gearbox.

SUSPENSION: Unique front struts and springs; Dimma rear shocks; lowered 7.2cm (2.8") all round.

BRAKES: Standard discs and pads.

WHEELS AND TYRES: Five-spoke — 8"x17" (20.3cmx43.2cm) wheels based on Compomotive ATs; 215/40 R17 Yokohama A510 rubber.

BODYWORK/PAINT: Steel front and rear Dimma wings, glassfibre front and back valance/bumpers, original shortened sills, painted in Curaçao Blue, Dimma fuel filler caps.

INTERIOR/ICE: Dimma retrimmed interior in cream leather; Panasonic CQ FX85 head unit, CX DP600 6-disc changer, CYMC-91 high performance active crossover; three CYM 9004 amps, one CYM 7002 amp, four EAB 301 12" (30.5cm) subs, four EAB REV4 mid-bass, two EAB REV6 mids and ST21 tweeters.

FORD ESCORT COSWORTH WRC

Snow White Charger

Snow White Charger

TALK TO MAX POWER WRITER Jon Walsh about this Escort Cosworth and he'll tell you it's the greatest cover car ever. The Scouser has a point: despite the Skyline's awesome power, this Escort has an even more impressive pedigree, that of the World Rally Championship and a bloke called Kankkunen.

The Skyline GTR made an impressive touring car, and won a few races in the Japanese GT championship, but a rally car will eat it over all sorts of surfaces, like, er, ice. And the Skyline is probably a little too big and heavy to ever cut it in the WRC. Besides, this Escort is British through-and-through, so it must be superior to that rice-burning garbage from the land of the rising sun, eh? Walshy discovered this car at a Silverstone rallysprint even, where its owner, Marcus Dodd, was competing in a full-works rally Escort Cosworth. This, according to Marcus, is his 'shed', for everyday use. It was parked behind the team tent, covered in road grime and filth. Some shed this is!

The car you see here is as near as dammit a full-spec World Rally Car. The only thing the engine lacks is an anti-lag system. The rest of it has been fettled by Ford rally masters Mountune to full group A spec, with a modified head, bigger grey injectors, Garrett T3 turbo, water injection and all the rest (see the spec panel). The result, when allied to a fully stripped out body shell, full works suspension and awesome group A tarmac-spec brakes, is stupendous performance all round.

'It's the scariest car I've ever been in,' says Walshy. 'Marcus was driving and floored the throttle a few hundred yards before we

Snow Whit

went into a roundabout. You know how urban roundabouts are quite heavily cambered, which sort of leaves a ridge on the way in and out. Well, we got airborne on the way in, and flew for a long way on the exit. The engine was on the limiter both times. Into, through, and out of tight corners, that car was flipping unbelievable'.

Yes, that's a full Escort WRC front end on Marcus' car, with a WRC rear spoiler at the back to match. Both work hard at keeping the Scort attached to the ground at high speed. And inside, it's stripped out to Group A spec too, with the full works carbon dash. With all this, it's easy to overlook the fact that it's running on 18in wheels. This car is indeed the dog's bollocks.

Snow White Charger

Max Fax

ENGINE: 1998cc, 16-valve; turbocharged Cosworth; Group 'A' cylinder head gasket, Group 'A' Mountune Eprom and Pectel board engine management system c/w water injection, but no antilag strategy, grey injectors, 3-bar map sensor, Group 'A' fuel pump within standard tank, Champion c57 spark plugs, Garrett T3 turbo with 360-degree thrust bearing, cut-back exhaust wheel, quick release Group 'A' turbo housing, Group 'A' actuator, Group 'N' engine mounts, free-flow motorsport airfilter; Scorpion stainless steel 7.2cm (2.8") straight-through exhaust system – all protected by a Kevlar sump guard.

TRANSMISSION: AP Racing Group 'A' paddle clutch; gearbox – Group 'N' Osbourne MT75 gear kit, quick shift gear linkage, uprated centre viscous coupling (50nm), Group 'N' mounting brackets; front differential – Group 'N' thick-walled casing with steel base gasket, no limited slip; rear differential – standard 16.8cm (7") casing with uprated viscous coupling (180nm), shoot peened gears, Group 'N' mounting brackets.

SUSPENSION: Front – Bilstein coilover dampers with Eibach 5.4cm (2") 38nm springs, standard anti-roll-bar with polyurethane bushes, rear beam mounting support plates, steel strut brace.

BRAKES: (Based on Group 'A' tarmac spec) Group 'A' adjustable pedalbox with dashboard-mounted adjuster, hydraulic handbrake, Goodridge brake lines running through inside of car, AP 600 brake fluid, no servo, no ABS; front – AP 4-pot racing calipers, AP alloy bell complete with 8-groove vented 315mm rotors, carbon metallic pads, Goodridge brake hoses; rear – AP 4-pot racing calipers, AP alloy bell complete with 8-groove vented 285mm rotors, carbon metallic pads.

WHEELS AND TYRES: Compomotive seven-spoke – 8"x18" (20.3cmx45.7cm) alloy wheels with Falken FK04GRBeta 225/40 18 tyres all round.

BODYWORK: Ford Escort WRC front bumper/spoiler/splitter, Ford Escort WRC front grille and surround, quad lamp conversion, Ford Escort WRC rear spoiler, windscreen wipers converted to LHD spec, RS2000 FR specs radiator – which looks like an intercooler, but isn't.

INTERIOR: Dashboard converted to lefthand drive, works carbonfibre dashboard panels, Recaro ex-works carbon-kevlar driver's seat, all other seats in leather, Momo dished suede steering wheel, alloy gearknob, adjustable pedalbox, hydraulic handbrake in cassette storage compartment.

ICE: Alpine head unit and 6-disc changer.

SECURITY: Tons.

PERFORMANCE: Max power – 380bhp.

CHAPTER 2
TOP TOTTY

We continue life on Planet Max with a
look at the top totty to have graced the
magazine's pages in the last year...

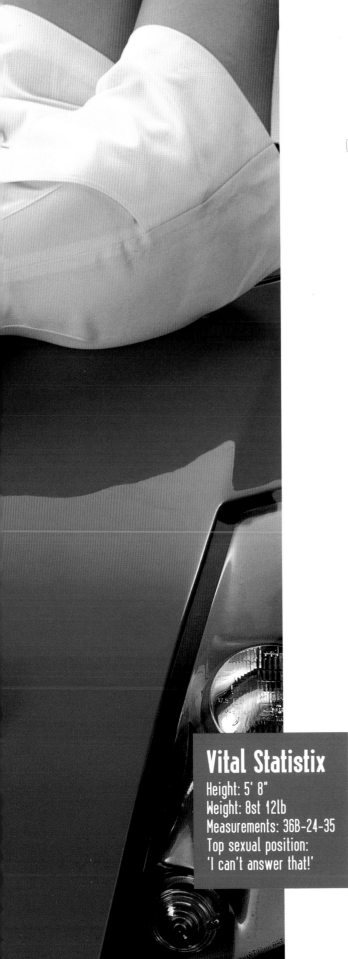

Taking Aleeka
Pure (Hand) Relief

THE FIRST FABULOUS filly out of the starting gate is the unusually named Aleeka, a 23-year-old blonde beauty from Philadelphia, USA who has now moved to London – good news for anyone south of Watford.

Aleeka is currently fella-less – even better news! If you want to ride this filly, you have to be laidback or sing to her and keep her happy with a ready supply of Marlboro Lights. 'I don't eat breakfast, so I'll settle for a man in my bed and a ciggy,' she drawls. Her ideal man, in case you were wondering – no, we didn't think you were – is Johnny Depp. And if you ever get close enough to nuzzle Aleeka, concentrate on her neck, 'cos that's her most erogenous zone.

When she lived in Philly, Aleeka and her mates had an unusual car game. 'It's called Chinese Fire Drill. Basically, you and your friends drive through town, then at each set of traffic lights you jump out and swap cars. The things is, you do it naked. You get some very surprised looks.' Now you know why it's called the city of brotherly love! Perhaps they should think of renaming it the city of sisterly love, since Aleeka readily admits, 'I've done naughtier things with women than I have with men.' And her choice for a lesbo lovefest would be Drew Barrymore. No slouch herself when it comes to sapphic sex, Drew once confessed, 'Do I like women sexually? Yes, I do. Totally. When I was younger I went with a lot of women. I don't think there's anything wrong with that. I fool around with women. I love a woman's body and think that a woman and a woman together is just as beautiful as a man and a woman.'

You've seen her bod, you know her views on sex (she drinks Becks, by the way), what else could you possibly want to know (apart from her phone number)? Oh, dear Aleeka, do you have a party trick?
'I can smoke a cigarette between my toes.' Fuck, agility as well!

We'll take Aleeka anytime, anyplace, anywhere!

Vital Statistix
Height: 5' 8"
Weight: 8st 12lb
Measurements: 36B-24-35
Top sexual position:
'I can't answer that!'

Turpin's Hotpot
Tasty, Tasty, Very, Very Tasty

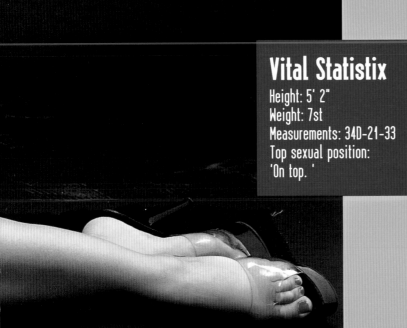

N EXT UP IS Liverpudlian lovely Debbie Turpin. 21-year-old Debs hails from the land that brought us Cilla Black, Ken Dodd and his Diddymen, Gerry & The Pacemakers and Bar Brookie's Jacqui Dixon – a businesswoman with so much savvy that the only way she could keep the café going was by having a surrogate baby for money! Still, one look at Debs and you could forgive the city anything – well, almost!

Debbie is a girl who speaks her mind, especially on matters of an intimate nature. Not only does she insist that size does matter, but she wants her blokes to measure up both widthways and lengthways! Little does she know how well the readers of Max Power can rise to that challenge.

If you wanted to cop off with our Debbie, then buying her some diamonds wouldn't go amiss. She obviously believes that diamonds are a girl's best friend. Oh, and some other tips: buy her some Chanel clothing, wear Possession aftershave, Calvin Klein clobber, drive a VW Polo, kiss her neck and ears and don't forget to be an Italian called Lee. Are you sure about that last bit, Debs, old girl?

Not only disloyalty to our great nation there, but there's also a touch of disloyalty to her home city; her favourite soap is not our Brookside but the depressingly dreary EastEnders. Still, when Debbie's around, who the fuck is going to give a toss about TV?

Vital Statistix

Height: 5' 2"
Weight: 7st
Measurements: 34D-21-33
Top sexual position:
'On top. '

Yummy Yasmin
All Right My Love

OFF TO THE WILDS of Surrey and leafy Richmond for 25-year-old Yasmin who, some would say, is here under false pretences. Here she is stuck in a car book, yet the lovely lass can't even drive! 'I don't really need a car. I usually walk on a night out with the girls,' she says revealingly. 'We start in a restaurant, head for a few bars and end up in a club. If I can get away with it, I'll drink champagne all night. If not, then I'll just slum it on lager'.

Yasmin has a musical ear and the rest of her ain't bad either. 'When I was about 3 years old, our neighbours were having a party and in the middle of the night I just got up and started singing Abba's Dancing Queen'. So what kind of music gets Yasmin strutting her stuff these days? 'Dance, house and 1980s' stuff is my thing. I don't mind Vivaldi's Four Seasons either'.

Showbiz obviously runs in Yasmin's blood. As well as gracing a certain page in a certain national newspaper, she has also done television with Mr Showbiz himself, Bruce Forsyth.

Didn't she do well!

Vital Statistix
Height: 5' 4"
Weight: 7st 6lb
Measurements: 36-22-34
Top sexual position:
'Yeah, right!'

Kaja Wunder Woman!

THE MOST EXOTIC of our fabulous five is Kaja Wunder, who was born and bred in Estonia which used to be part of the U.S.S.R, and which first entered that nirvana of naffness the Eurovision Song Contest, in 1994. Their most successful entry was in 1996, by the way, when they finished fifth with Kaelakee Hääl sung by Ivo Linna and Maarja-Liis Ilus – just thought you might like to know. Oh well, suit yourself.

Kurvy Kaja defected eight years ago when the Berlin Wall was still in place. 'It was difficult to travel,' she explains. 'I had a tourist visa to go to Sweden. Once I got there I stayed and didn't go back. I was only 19 and an illegal immigrant. There was a real possibility that I might never see my family again.'

Kaja was a precocious little, well actually not so little, thing. 'I took my driving test at school. I got a professional licence, so I'm licensed to drive a taxi in Estonia.'

This beaut can even change a tyre, but as for fixing a mangled motor, 'I really don't have to. I just click my fingers and someone else does it.' This girl has her head screwed on. And talking of screwing, yes she has done it in a car. 'I think everybody has, haven't they?' (Must have been one fuck of a big car!) but she's never snogged another girl seriously.

Give it time, luv.

If you want to take her out and wunder, sorry wonder, about what drink to buy her then we'd recommend red wine, 'cos she gets drunk very quickly. Failing that, try a brown Polish vodka called Bison. This girl has hidden talents. 'I like to be appreciated for what I am. It's boring to only be wanted for your looks (Yes, we the staff of Max Power know how you feel!). I can knit, sew and I throw a mean hand grenade (!). I also speak six languages: English, Estonian, Russian, French, Swedish and Finnish'.

Kaja, you really are our Wunder Woman!

Vital Statistix
Height: 6'
Weight: 8st 10lb
Measurements: 36-26-36
Top sexual position:
'Classified information!'

Claire The Metal Maniac

SAVING THE BEST to last is something that former Miss America Vanessa Williams knows all about, and we are sure Van would appreciate Claire Peckham, our lovely Lincolnshire lass.

Claire, as well as being extraordinarily beautiful, also has a secret talent. She makes furniture out of lumps of metal. Yes, that's right – furniture out of lumps of metal. She has her own company called Metal Maniacs and they will make anything from a metal bed to a metal armchair to, well your imagination's the limit. Orders for furniture, c/o the publisher, will be passed on to her.

On the road front, Claire drives a souped-up 1951 Morris Minor Convertible which contains a 1500cc engine from an MG. 'Everyone's your friend in a Moggy, everyone wants to talk to you,' she laughs. 'In a TVR everyone thinks you're a show-off and gives you grief. The Moggy's pretty quick, though. It'll leave XR3s at the lights – and it corners really well.'

Cars were once nearly Claire's downfall. 'I was with my boyfriend in a car a few years back and we ran away from the police. We'd been street racing in a Mk2 Escort when the cops started chasing us. We got away and hid in a driveway until we thought it was safe. Then, as we drove out, who was coming along the road but the police car. We got caught and my boyfriend got banned.'

Claire is a very open (and we do mean open), game girl when it comes to porn. She's appeared in Mayfair, Penthouse and Playboy and although, 'I wouldn't do videos,' she does add, 'There's nothing wrong with watching a vid. I think it improves your sex life. I can (now) do things with my legs that other girls can't.'

Way to go, Claire-ikins!!

Vital Statistix

Height: 5' 8"
Weight: 7st 6lb
Measurements: 34C-24-35
(In case you're interested, Claire's birthday is 10 January, she's got size 6 feet, takes a size 10 dress and her inside leg measures 33".)
Top sexual position: 'All of them!'

Claire The Metal Maniac

CHAPTER 3
ICE IS NICE!

You've changed the wheels, altered the transmission, had the interior fitted out in the finest mahogany, put on solid gold windscreen wipers (well, perhaps not), but what have you forgotten? The fucking ICE of course! It's just as well we haven't. Here's the good stuff...

Cold as Ice

THE PANASONIC BMW 323I

YOU MIGHT WELL ask what good stuff ever came out of Norway? Fucking Norway! Snow. Reindeer. Father bloody Christmas – and this ultimate ICE demo car.

Panasonic Norway employ a guy called Bosse Langaas, who you can call Bo (it's a lot easier than trying to pronounce his name). Anyway, Bo had a little help from a fellow ICE head called Petter who is a dab hand at awesome ICE installs. They've designed a car with two systems and two head units.

In standard mode, the Beemer runs a whole lot of speakers you can see, and a shit load you can't. Bo and Peter have one of the two pairs of tweeters in the A-pillars. The trim work is so perfect you'd expect them to be a factory mod. The factory door locations have been ignored and there's been some hard work put into a pair of kick panel builds. These house a pair of 5" mids and the other two tweeters. To improve the imaging, the tweeters have been mounted on tiny aluminium struts so they sit directly in the middle of the mid-range speaker. This gives the impression the sound is coming from one source rather than two.

Look towards the dash and you'll see not one, but two headunits. There's a CQ-RDP855 CD/tuner which sits in the slot BMW made for it. But, there's another, altogether bigger head unit sitting just below it. The UK craze for double-DIN headunits has reached Norway and Bo hasn't disappointed. He specially imported a Panasonic CQ-AV150 direct from Japan to fit into the BMW so he could watch a few movies. Flash, or what? This is usually a cassette/tuner and LCD screen all in one, but not here. Fitting the complete AV150 into

the dash would have meant chopping great chunks out of the BMW heater system. Not an option, considering the complexity of the job. It was decided to mount the front panel in the dash and, via a massive amount of relays and wires, hide the head unit itself between the rear seat and the boot install. Of course, this makes inserting cassettes impossible so the AV-150 is reduced to a two function head unit, not three.

As if to make up for this, Bo and Petter have installed a Panasonic NV-HD610 DVD player and connected it to the AV150. DVD? Basically, DVD is short for Digital Verstile Disc. This is a disc which looks and feels exactly the same as a standard compact disc, but it contains a complete film. DVD players allow you to watch movies

on these shit-hot discs as well as play conventional CDs through them. The technology is still fairly new at the moment, but give it a year and it'll be up & running big time. There's already a few prototype in-car DVD players in existence, so expect DVD to take off big time. At the moment you'll have to make do with this, which just happens to be the first car in the world to be fitted with a fully functioning DVD player.

This car has the best of both worlds. A sexy sounding system to cruise around with and enough room to see some action on the back seat when you pull. Then, when you want to be really flash, you can whip out the back seat and plumb in an extra ten subs and four amps. Simple really.

Once connected up, the amps can be revealed thanks to a motorised amp rack. The rack is finished with perspex on both sides so you can ogle at the 9004's glorious heat sink, or the

Cold as Ice

ICE Spec
The Panasonic Norway BMW 323i

SOUND SOURCE: Panasonic CQ-RDP855 CD/tuner, Panasonic CQ-AV150 cassette/tuner/LCD screen linked to NV-HD610 home DVD player, 2x Panasonic DP-601 multi-changers (one per headunit).

AMPLIFICATION: Panasonic CY-MC9004 (powering the front 6" mids, 5" mids and two pairs of tweeters), Panasonic CY-MC9004 (powering the rear mids & 'daily use' sub) Show box – 4x Panasonic CY-M9004 (powering all 10 subs).

PROCESSORS: Panasonic CYMC-91 active crossover.

SPEAKERS: 4x Panasonic tweeters (two in kick builds, two in A-pillars), 4x Panasonic 5" (12.7cm) mids (two front & two rear), 2x Technics (R&D use only) 6" (15.2cm) mids (under dash), 1x Panasonic (prototype) 10" (25.4cm) sub for daily use (boot mounted), 'show box' holding 10x Panasonic 12" (30.5cm) subs (six mounted isobaric style, four mounted normally facing the front of the car). Panasonic & Technics are the same company, so now you know why the Technics stuff is in there. And no, you can't buy them over here.

CABLES: Phoenix Gold RCA speaker and power cables throughout.

POWER SUPPLY: Factory, with uprated battery.

Installed By: Bo and Petter at Peco Bild, Norway.

exposed innards at the back.

Sitting in the boot is a solitary 9004 taking pride of place. There's actually two, so the one you see mounted under the perspex is piggy-backing another amp. The lower amp is a bit like those in the motorised box and has the back removed so you can see its circuitry. Because you can't see it directly, Bo's motorised the rack and mounted a mirror to reflect the image towards you. Lift up the mirror and there you can see the DVD player in all its glory.

Also sitting in the boot is a second battery and charger system. This has a continuous cooling fan running to keep the charger cool. Rather than having an unsightly fan spinning in the floor, Bo and Peter have used a speaker grille as a cover. This also protects the fan blades from debris. Thanks to the split charger system, the car can crank it for ages without the worry of flattening the batteries.

A Reet Nice Chopper!

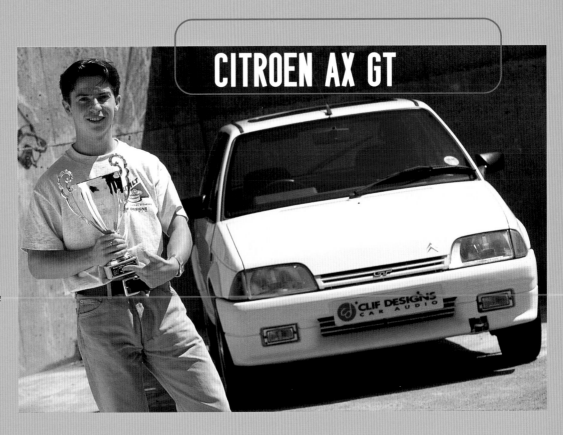

CITROEN AX GT

SUPER ICE AX owner Mark Gleeson is a lucky sod. He just happened to be on holiday in the Caribbean (which is jammy enough) when he spotted a duty free shop selling heaps & heaps of ICE. Top of his personal wanted list was a very bargain basement Rockford 60x2 amp. Normally retailing at £400, Mark only had to pay a measly £170. See, we told you he was a lucky sod!

Desperate to leave the sun-shine paradise that Viv Richards calls home, Mark couldn't wait until he got back to Blighty to install it. He did all the work himself.
'I put it down to all that time spent watching Blue Peter. The things you can do with sticky back plastic is amazing'. Yeah, thanks Mark. He converted the standard AX GT into a fantastic ICE monster using a stack of MDF, black vinyl, per-spex, Scosche cables and Clif Design speakers.

Mark's choice of Clif Design subs made a few people question his grip on reality. He gave them a few home truths, like the price for starters... they weigh in at a paltry £130 each. You might only get a pressed cage, but the sound quality is fantastic. Their thump is strong enough to rattle the back teeth of the hardest ICE freak.

With everything installed, Mark took a trip to Sterling ICE to have the car set-up. Top geezer John sat the RTA meter in the car and shot some pink noise through the system. The system scored a

A Reet Nice Chopper!

mediocre 24 points. With a possible top score of 40, the result didn't leave him a happy bunny. An in-depth look at the results pointed to the tweeters and x-overs being the weak point. The Clif Design mids were incredible but the Cerwin Vega Stealth tweeters and Cerwin Vega x-overs were letting the side down big time. John had to convince Mark to splash out on the Clif Design tweeters and x-overs to compliment the existing mids.

With the new stuff bolted into place, the pink noise treatment was given a go. Hey presto, it's a magic 34 on the RTA and the system wasn't even set up yet. John and Mark jumped up and down and kissed each other and decided to spend the rest of the day setting it all up. Mark's Alpine ERE-G180 graphic is as basic as you could get for a competition car, but the lads got stuck in, regardless. The result of the hard graft was a toe-tingling score of 37. Result! Mark was right chuffed.

At the moment, the weak point of the system is the Scosche line driver. It's a little £50 gadget which boosts the signal from the head unit to the amps and means they don't have to work so hard. The only problem is, the line-driver ups the signal, which means that any noise coming from the head unit is also boosted. Unfortunately, this is a trait of the cheaper units, so Mark plans to bin it soon. Also for the chop is the Alpine equaliser. It's simply not up to the job, so he's going to splash some cash on an Audio Control EQX-Series 2. This bit of kit happens to be a 13-band per channel equaliser with a built in line-driver.

RTA

The RTA meter checks how smooth the frequency response of the system is. Pink noise is a bit like the sound from the TV in Poltergeist, you know, that fuzzy scrambled stuff. Anyway, the RTA meter can measure the levels of pink stuff coming through all the subs, mids and tweeters. A nice level response gives a fairly flat line and, hence, a nice RTA score. A line full of troughs and peaks leaves a little to be desired on the set-up front. There's a possible 40 to be had, which is halved and added to the total score.

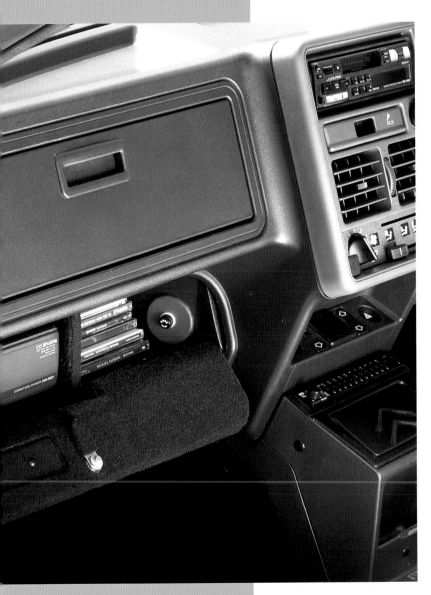

SOUND SOURCE: Alpine TDM 7532R cassette/tuner head unit with Alpine CHM-S601, 6-disc changer.

AMPLIFICATION: Front: Rockford Fosgate Punch 60x2 amp running at 4ohms. Rear: Rockford Fosgate Punch 40i DSM amp running at 2ohms.

PROCESSORS: Alpine ERE-G180 graphic equaliser, Scosche line-driver.

SPEAKERS: Front: Clif Design CDS-1 tweeters and Clif Design CCD-6 mids controlled by Clif Design Moducross MX x-overs. Rear: two Clif Design DVC-10 10" subs.

CABLES: Scosche throughout.

POWER SUPPLY: Standard Citroen stuff.

CAP: Caliber stiffening cap – 1 farad.

NICE INSTALL BITS: Colour-coded cooling fans, split speed fan controller (varies the speed of the fans according to the temperature of the amps, lots of points there), cables recessed into trenches in the MDF, a nice colour coded tool kit.

PERFORMANCE: A jolly decent 37 on the RTA meter.

Stroll On? Ride On!!

BMW Z3

I N THE WORLD of Max, a car isn't a car without a credible sound system and this Z3 was a classic victim of neglect by the manufacturers. That is, until it was sent to England where it fell into the hands of ICE guru, Matthew Robins, owner of Westcliff-based Ride On! He's been around the ICE scene about as long as Joan Collins has been in showbiz. Maff was the guy responsible for setting up Sterling ICE but now he's moved on and the Z3 is the first success from his new company Ride On!

Matthew's got big plans for Ride-On! 'We're planning to launch a number of Vehicle Enhancement Programmes (VEP) in the future and we need to break away from the previous organisation. We're still involved with the other Stirling ICE branches but Ride-On! will specialise in the areas we enjoy most'. VEP? Take your new car to Maff and have it converted to a Ride On! Special Edition. The basic programmes available include ICE and security, but they'll go further to include imported wheel packages, suspension and complete interiors to create a car worthy of the Ride On! logo.

Ride On! Head Installer, John Gaymer, proves with the Z3 that you can have great sound in an open top two-seater. John & Maff tried a series of listening tests in the Z3 using a variety of positions to find the best place to mount the tweeters. It turned out to be slap bang in the middle of the A-pillars. John stripped them out with a sharp knife and grafted in some CD Technology tweeters. The finish is comparable with BMWs very own factory fit.

Working with the tweeters are the matching 5" mids. All part of the CD Technologies HD-52 component kit, they come with a great looking pair of crossovers which John has placed on show in the boot. The mids are mounted into the factory speaker positions in the footwells. No door builds here though, as stealth is the order of the day. They provide a nice amount of bass, bringing it forward in the car, but real bass is supplied by a 10" sub mounted in the parcel shelf. The 10" Velodyne

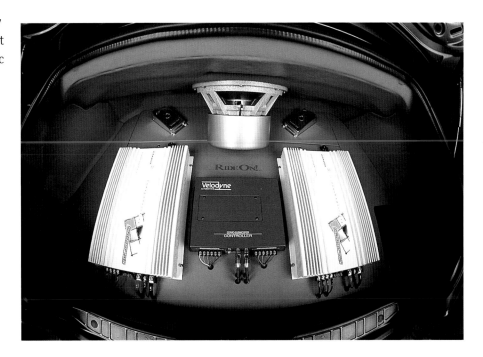

Stroll On? Ride On!

sub is a techy's heaven. The one used in the Zed is called a DF10SC. That's because DF stands for Distortion Free, 10 is because it's a 10 incher and SC means it's Servo Controlled. Simple, eh? There's a little bit which we've overlooked here; it's distortion free. That's no distortion, at all, ever. That's 'cos the output for the sub is taken directly from the head unit and, rather than going straight to the amp, is fed directly into the Velodyne control unit. It's at this point that the control unit monitors the initial input signal to see what it's doing. The unit then outputs to any amplifier using RCA cables. The amp does it's job as per usual. The amplified signal is then fed straight into the sub. Then things get really high tech. The sub is fitted with a cone mounted accelerometer which is linked to the control unit. This monitors the sub woofer output and the control unit compares it to the original signal direct from the headunit. There's also a second acceler-ometer which monitors the car's motion and road noise etc. Any differences between all three signals are compensated for by the control unit and ensures good quality, distortion free bass. I hope you're paying attention, 'cos we'll be asking questions later.

The power stations in this system are a pair of Crossfire amps. Pushing out 200w RMS each, one CFA402 is running the compo-nents, the second is bridged to power the Velodyne. Not being frightfully expensive means the amps are very impressive.

ICE Spec
The Ride On! BMW Z3

SOUND SOURCE: Kenwood KDC-9050R (4v output) CD/tuner.

AMPLIFICATION: Crossfire CFA402 2x100RMS (powering the mids & tweeters), Crossfire CFA402 (bridged to power the Velodyne).

PROCESSORS: Nothing, unless you include the Velodyne controller.

SPEAKERS: CD Technologies HD-52 5¼" mid & tweeter components, 1x Velodyne DF10SC 10" reactived sub.

CABLES: Scosche RCA, speaker and power cables throughout.

POWER SUPPLY: Factory.

CAP: N/A.

INSTALLED BY: John Gaymer at Ride On!

NICE INSTALL BITS: That sub.

PERFORMANCE: N/A.

Vorsprung Durch Something Or Other

BMW 325i

RACING DYNAMICS

RGY 379

VorsPrung Durch Something

THE WELL HUNG, low slung bass in this car is provided by three JL Audio 12W6 subs. These subs will set you back around 300 sovs. These subs can growl as low as you like. Boom Boom Bass isn't a particularly great CD, but it is great for demonstrating the depth these JLs can drop to. They are pummelled to death on a regular basis by the awesome power of the boot mounted Soundstream amp. A hunk of a Class A 10.0 amplifier, this Soundstream is bridged and reckoned to pump out an awesome 1000w RMS.

However, there is always a price to pay for the good stuff, as Divine Brown once told Hugh Grant. The JLs need backing up with a sensible power supply. In fact, the whole install needs help. Prestige have installed a pair of Rockford Fosgate stiffening capacitors. Should the big bass tunes kick in, the amps will start draining the power supply big time. The caps store enough juice to feed the amps and as soon as the bass cools off, the caps have time to store up more power again.

At the front of the car we encounter two massive door builds housing the mid-range speakers. They're a fantastic piece of kit with a kevlar cone, full-on glorious rubber surround and a heavyweight die cast chassis. They can be used as a nice mid-bass cum bass unit but they're awesome as a mid-range driver. They're not cheap at £280 a pair, but the sound is fantastic. They're housed in a mixture of original BMW door card, MDF, fibreglass and Dynamat, all topped off with a generous helping of alcantara. This stuff, as you know, is a synthetic suede. It costs a packet and, unlike real suede, comes off a perfect roll. No imperfections there.

Holding hands with the mids and nicely filling in the top end is a pair of Image Dynamics CD-1 horns. The fact they are horns and not your standard 'bolt in the dash' tweeters means it has to be a professional installation job to get them in any car. Positioning and the angle they sit at are both crucial. The horns have a vinyl covered MDF frame on their fronts. Powering the horns and the mids are a pair of Rockford Fosgate Punch 200 amps. Rockford don't produce these amps anymore but the owner enjoyed them so much, he insisted on them being used in the re-vamped install. To upgrade them, the heat sinks were stripped and polished to match the new Soundstream amp. Along with the red alcantara and red detailing on the DSMs, the finish carries through quite nicely.

In fact, most of the kit sits in the boot: all three amps, the Phoenix Gold EQ-230, three thumping JL subs, the Alpine 12-disc changer and the two Rockford caps. It's a tight squeeze but it seems to work quite well. The whole lot is capped off with a sheet of perspex (so perfect you can hardly see it in the photos) and a black alcantara covered frame.

The BMW sits unfeasibly low thanks to a Racing Dynamics set-up.

Other

Originally on 16" alloys, the car had trouble getting over manhole covers, crisp packets and squashed hedgehogs. The 17" OZ alloys have raised the car a bit, which means it only has trouble with sleeping policemen. The stainless steel Scorpion exhaust has had extra supports added in defence of anything it may drive over. Which probably happens when he's too busy watching the telly. The Alpine CVA-1000R is a monitor/tuner capable of taking inputs from a TV tuner, navigation system and even a video. It also has the optional TV tuner added and a 12-disc changer plumbed in. The touch of a button has the blank face sliding out and, hey presto, it's a monitor. Of course, things are never that easy. What with the shape of the BMW dash and the positioning of the indicator stalk, the monitor used to knock against it, meaning the screen couldn't be viewed. Prestige cut and shut it and now the Alpine glides out with ease, and not a stalk in sight. Cool.

ICE Spec
BMW 325i ICE car

SOUND SOURCE: Alpine CVA-1000R monitor/tuner head unit, Alpine TV tuner, Alpine CHA-1204 12-disc changer.

AMPLIFICATION: Rockford Fosgate Punch 200 DSM 2x100WRMS amp (powering dash mounted Image Dynamics horns), Rockford Fosgate Punch 200 DSM 2x100WRMS amp (powering door mounted Prestige mids), Soundstream Class A 10.0 amp (bridged to power all subs).

PROCESSORS: Phoenix Gold AX-406A crossover, Phoenix Gold EQ-230 30-band graphic equaliser.

SPEAKERS: Image Dynamics CD-1e horns (dash), Prestige sourced 6" mid-range (doors), three JL Audio 12W6 12" boxed subs.

CABLES: Phoenix Gold speaker and power cables throughout.

POWER SUPPLY: Standard, with Optima battery in factory position

CAP: 2x 1 farad Rockford Fosgate capacitors.

INSTALLED BY: The boys at Prestige.

NICE INSTALL BITS: Two pieces of Alcantara covering a whole door.

Huet's Your Lot!

GOLF GTI

TAKE ONE award-winning car and put it in the more than capable hands of Huet Car Audio, among the top five acclaimed masters of ICE in Britain, and what do you get? The ultimate Golf GTi, that's what!

In 1995 it took the Sound Off series by storm. It was European Champion in 1996. Now the Huets are back to add to their tally with even more modifications. As Frank Spencer might have said, "Every day in every way it gets better and better".

The first thing you notice is that... erm, nothing seems to have changed. But take a gander around and the differences become apparent. First there's the head unit – the Alpine 7939 CD-Max has no internal amps but a whopping 4v output give this a pure sound and make it the number one choice on the Sound Off circuit.

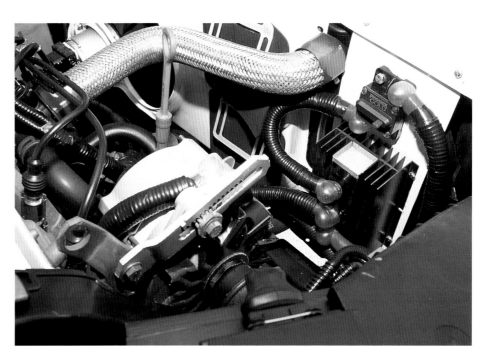

The most ingenious change though, is the new location for the multi-changer. It's not in the usual places – glove compartment, boot, under the passenger seat. No. These devious Huet chaps have devised a sneaky place. The dashboard mounted air vents have a micro-switch behind the stock-looking control. A small motor pushes down the 'vents' to reveal the multi-changer. The bank of 'stock' switches in the dash have a few strange markings on them, one being an 'eject' symbol. Flick it and the cartridge shoots out. The rest of the switches are also functional.

Another clever addition by the lads at Huet is the Sony Mini-8 install. Another dashboard switch operates the motorised drawer which also has an LED temperature gauge mounted on it. This is linked to a temperature sensor in the amp rack. If it becomes too hot, then two linear fans kick-in, one pulls hot air out and one pushes cool air in. They both vent through the boot floor towards the tarmac.

In the centre console is also the Alpine Ai-Net monitor. It's connected to the Mini-8 video player. However, if you think you can watch the box and drive at the same time, you're wrong. The

Huet's Your Lot!

ever safety-conscious Huets have added a micro switch to the hand brake so the screen only works with the brake on.

There are only five speakers in the Golf, but all are well powered and provide a glorious sound. There's a pair of Image Dynamics CD-2 horns carefully grafted into the dash. This is anything but simple to do. The fuse box had to be relocated about 7" higher than its original position. Huets have also used a VW spec vinyl to re-trim the horn surrounds, providing the stock look.

Further down you see the 6" Phoenix Gold PG-ZCS6 speakers in a set of kick panel builds. To install these the pedals had to be removed, modified and re-fitted to enable them to fit. Like fitting the horns, the job wasn't easy but it does mean the mids are well angled for sounding great.

The bass is courtesy of a JL Audio JL-12W6 12" sub. This has been housed in a fibreglass and MDF-sealed enclosure, the size of which brings the most out of the sub. The box sinks deep into the rear quarter panels and is nicely finished in that VW vinyl. To stop the panels rattling, and to improve the overall sound of the car, over £1000 worth of sound deadening has been employed. The car was totally gutted inside until all that remained was the paint. Dynamat, a totally excellent sound deadening material which is like a 5mm thin carpet of marzipan, has been stuck to every part of the car.

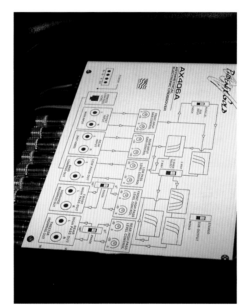

The roof and floor have been covered and the doors were given double helpings. If you go outside and tap your car door, you'll get a tinny sound. Tap a door treated to Dynamat and you've got a happy, dull thud. It means the panels won't move and won't absorb the sound within the car.

In the boot the ZX-200 Phoenix Gold amps have been mounted the right way up, but to add a bit of interest the ZX-350 has been mounted upside down. This meant that the printing would be upside down. The lads overcame this by having one specially screen printed. A custom neon, a speciality of Huets, highlights the amps and is operated by the boot switch. The amp rack is on a pair of motorised sliders which tilt the unit up to reveal an inlaid tool kit and easy access to the spare wheel. The motors are controlled by an extra channel on the Clifford remote.

The whole ICE system is powered by a Lightning battery. This has been encased in a steel box and its position has meant the fuel tank fixings had to be moved. It's juiced by a very special Huets split charger system with the help of a Lightening 1.5 farad capacitor.

We're going to keep an eye on the Huets Golf and see what happens. It's sure to be fascinating.

ICE Spec

Chris Huet's Golf GTi

SOUND SOURCE: Alpine CDA-7939R CD-Max CD/tuner, Alpine TVA-MO13P monitor, Alpine VPA-P004 monitor processor, Sony Mini-8 U5E video player.

AMPLIFICATION: One Phoenix Gold ZX-350 (2x37watt RMS) powering the JL sub, two Phoenix Gold ZX-200 amps (2x18watt RMS) powering the horns & mids (All at 12v).

PROCESSORS: Phoenix Gold EQ-230 Nrd octave equaliser, Phoenix Gold AX-406 3-way cross-over, Phoenix Gold LPL-44 bass trimming device.

SPEAKERS: Front: dash mounted Image Dynamics CD-2 horns and kick panel mounted Phoenix Gold PG-ZCS6, 6" mid bass units. Rear: sealed box mounted JL Audio JL-12W6, 12" sub.

CABLES: Phoenix Gold throughout.

POWER SUPPLY: Golf diesel alternator, Golf diesel battery up front, Huets own split-charger system linked to Lightening Cell rear battery.

CAP: Lightening 1.5 farad capacitor.

INSTALLED BY: Huets In-Car Audio of Hove.

NICE INSTALL BITS: Where do you start? Remote control sensors in the rear view mirror, multi-changer install, Mini-8 install, sub level controller aka the cigar lighter, smart use of factory switches, motorised stuff (always a winner), upside-down screen printing on the ZX-350 amp to match the other amps, custom neons, tool kit, etc.

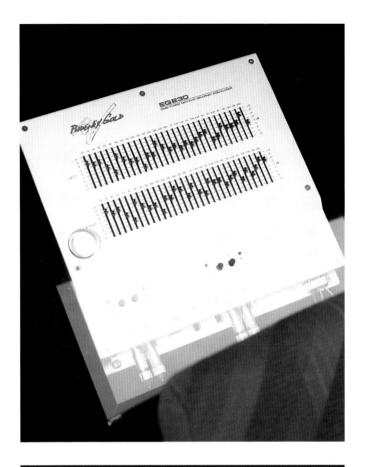

Stock? Custom? Huh?

In SCA terms, stock is where the speakers would have been if the manufacturers had known what they were doing. Custom is making a song-and-dance of the speaker install. Thing is though, the install can be stock and custom. Confused? Don't be. On the Huets car the head unit is a stock install 'cos it's where it's meant to be. The Amps are stock and custom 'cos Huets have used black vinyl which matches the VW material, they're seen as stock (i.e. If VW had installed three amps, they'd probably be in the same place), and they're custom 'cos of the motorised stuff, neons and perspex.

A Cavalier Attitude

A Cavalier Attitude

VAUXHALL CAVALIER

JAMES WHEELER has been grabbed by the ICEing bug. Five years ago he bought a diesel Vauxhall Cavalier and three years ago began to have the car modified to his own very precise specifications.

With the help of those veterans of modification – the Huets – he installed two USD Waveguides. The glovebox was sacrificed on the passenger side, and the bonnet release was 'modified' to fit the equipment on the driver's side. Integration with the car's dashboard and existing vinyl is important in Sound Off terms. Matching the horns are a pair of USD 8" mid-range speakers. These are fitted into Huets' own design of kick panel builds. The front end is powered by a Phoenix Gold ZX450 amp.

The install has only six speakers in the whole car. Its layout is clean and the two JL Audio subs fitted into a 2 cubic foot box give a crisp sound. The box doesn't seem that big, but that's because the back panel is recessed into the bodywork using fibreglass, MDF and a big hammer. These are powered by a Phoenix Gold ZX500 amp. This is backed up by a pair of Lightning Cap capacitors which help when the bass kicks.

The front of the car is a bit special. We've mentioned the Waveguides installation and the Huets mids installation, but not the TBAt. It takes the signal from the Alpine 7939, which is already producing a 4 volt output and boosts it to around 9 volts. Not only that, but the TBAt converts the head units RCA output to a balanced output. Instead of using RCA cables to carry the signal from the front of the car through to the boot area, the TBAt uses two telephone type cables. There are 8 or 9 volts running through the cable and this is a relatively huge signal. At best, you may only get a 4v signal from a pukka head unit. Signal loss through the cable length is tiny because the signal is so big. The main difference is the way the two use an earth. An RCA cable uses the outer cable as the earth. The same

earth is used for the left and right channels and basically connects to the car's chassis. One of the problems with an RCA cable is it can act as a capacitor, storing current in the sleeving between the positive and negative cables. The balanced option uses the same signal but along with a clean negative produced by the head unit. The main advantages of using a balanced line output is the lack of interference, compared with RCA, and good signal transfer properties. In an ideal world, the head unit would be supplying a balanced output of its own, it's a much cleaner and purer signal. With the TBAt being so close to the head unit, loss in sound quality down the RCA cable linking the two is minimal. The TBAt does have the added advantage of adjustability. You can control its output voltage to the taste of the amp or EQ it's supplying. Some amps don't like massively high input voltage, so having that adjustable luxury is ideal.

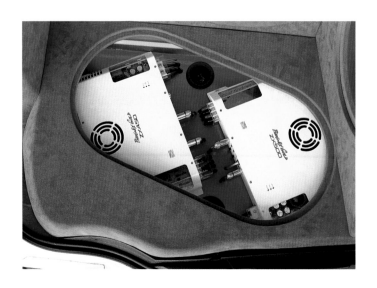

ICE Spec
James Wheeler's ICE car

SOUND SOURCE: Alpine 7939 CD-Max CD/tuner

AMPLIFICATION: Phoenix Gold ZX450 (powering the front horns and mids), Phoenix Gold ZX500 (powering the JL Audio subs).

PROCESSORS: Phoenix Gold TBAt and Phoenix Gold EQ-230.

SPEAKERS: 2x dashboard-mounted USD Waveguides, 2x kick panel mounted USD 8" (20.3cm) mid-range drivers, 2x boot mounted JL Audio 10W6 subs.

CABLES: Phoenix Gold speaker and power cables throughout.

POWER SUPPLY: Optima 850 (red top).

CAP: Two 1 farad Lightening Cap capacitors.

INSTALLED BY: Huets In-Car Audio of Hove.

NICE INSTALL BITS: Toolkit (winner), micro neon around TBAt for £100.

The Devil's Idle Hands

LAMBORGHINI DIABLO

The Devil's Idle Hands

AS IF HAVING a Lamborghini wouldn't satisfy most blokes, some just have to go one step further. Phil Leech is one such geezer. He believes power is everything. You'd think 530bhp under his right foot would be enough, but no. Phil has added more power in the form of Rockford's finest ICE. There may be only five speakers in his Diablo, but there are four rocking Punch amps powering them.

The signal is produced by Rockford's Max Award winning RFE-8140 head unit and then processed and controlled by a Rockford EPX-2. It controls the crossover points, bass levels and all sorts of shit. The signal is then split between four amps. The bass signal goes to two Punch 40.2 amps which power the 8" subs twin voice coils. On full flap, these amps give out 175watts each, which means the Rockford 8" is receiving a pure, throbbing 350watts. There's only one 8" sub in the Diablo but it's punchy and solid and it drops a lot lower than you'd expect. The best thing is, that it has two voice coils which can be powered separately, like they are in this system.

For the mid and the top-end, a Rockford RFR-1614 component set-up is used. These are housed in some groovy Alcantara/alloy door builds. The car was designed to be a show

car from the start, so the door builds were highlighted with alloy panels without any speaker grilles to cover the Rockford stuff. Each door has its own amp to power it. The two Punch 60.2 amps are mounted behind each seat and produce 270watts each. The amps are run bridged/in mono. This means the signal from the EPX-2 is split, the left channel goes to one amp and the right channel goes to the other. It's a tiny bit extravagant running so many amps, but that's the type of motor this is. OTT, but totally fab and groovy.

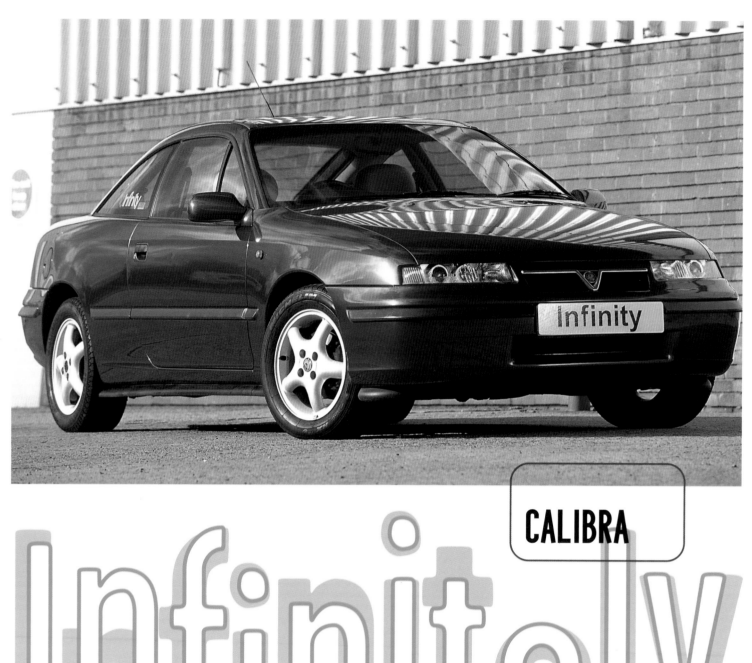

CALIBRA

Infinitely
The best

AT FIRST GLANCE, this Calibra is no different from any other. But when you take a second look, you notice the pair of 8" subs in the foot wells. So what?, you may ask, but look again – this time at the driver's side. The pedals haven't been moved and you can still press them all the way without touching the floor or speaker. Fitting an 8" sub somewhere like that is impressive because lots of metal work and fabrication needs to be done plus you have to be careful not to foul the engine's moving parts. This car didn't need any of that work done to it. It's had a pair of these new Infinity UniPlane speakers fitted. From front to back, including the grille, magnet and cone, the 8" versions measure 33mm. The 6" mid-bass and 6" two ways are 31.5 mm and the 4" is a wafer-thin mint at 22.5mm. Being this thin makes their installation possibilities almost limitless, meaning that you can bring a whole new sound stage to the front of your car. Fitting the Infinity Kappa UniPlane speakers in the front lets you bring the bass forward in the car.

The mounting depth isn't the only thing which is striking about these speakers, there is also the weight to consider. The speaker chassis is made of plastic, not metal and the magnet is tiny. These things are ultra light and just the job if this is a priority when considering the install for your modified motor.

Thanks to a Kappa 12" sub seated in a sealed box and bolted to the floor, you get more than enough bass. This means the music is at a reasonable level, not too loud, and yet the mid-bass effect is awesome. That is not to say this UniPlane stuff is the be-all-and-end-all of bass. This is mid-bass we're talking about and it ain't going to blow your feet off the pedals when you're driving. What it will do is bring oodles of quality, mid-bass to the front of your motor. Even a small amount of bass upfront will feel like loads as it balances out with the rear. Thanks to the magic mounting depths, you can mount an 8" speaker pretty much wherever you like. With only a 33mm mounting depth, you can fit your 8" UniPlane driver into the roof lining. If your sun visors are 22.5mm thick, you could even stick a 4" UniPlane in there.

Anatomy of a UniPlane

When Infinity created these speakers, they knew what they were doing. The magnets are very small and light and the cones are made from APC (Acrylic Polymer Gel - that's the green stuff) which is said to be very strong compared with your average, common or garden speaker cones. Reversing the voice coil and magnet assembly and having a stronger cone means Infinity can do without a spider. Basically, instead of having the magnet at the bottom of a cone, the cone's been flipped over and the magnet sat in the inside.

ICE Spec
The Infinity UniPlane Calibra

SOUND SOURCE: Alpine 7939R CD-Max.

AMPLIFICATION: 2x Infinity 52a (2x 50w at 4 ohms) powering the UniPlane 62f speakers, 1x Infinity 102a (2x 100w at 4 ohms) powering the 80f mid-bass, 1x Infinity 102a (bridged to 1x 300w at 4 ohms) powering the Kappa 120w.ib (12" sub).

PROCESSORS: 2x Audio Control EQT equalizers, one per channel.

SPEAKERS: Front: 2x Kappa UniPlane 80f (8" mid-bass speakers), 2x Kappa UniPlane 62f (6" two-way speakers); back: Infinity Kappa 120w.br 12" sub in sealed enclosure.

CABLES: Varied.

POWER SUPPLY: Factory power supply with plug-in for show/static use.

CAP: N/A.

INSTALLED BY: Andy Lee, the in-house installation pro at Gamepath.

NICE INSTALL BITS: The 8" mid-bass speakers.

The best

CHAPTER 4
CRUISIN'

Each month Max Power invades your town to check out the cars, ogle the totty and generally annoy the Old Bill. Join us for a cruise down memory lane and relive the classic burn outs, unpleasant moonies and exquisite scenes of birds snogging each other...

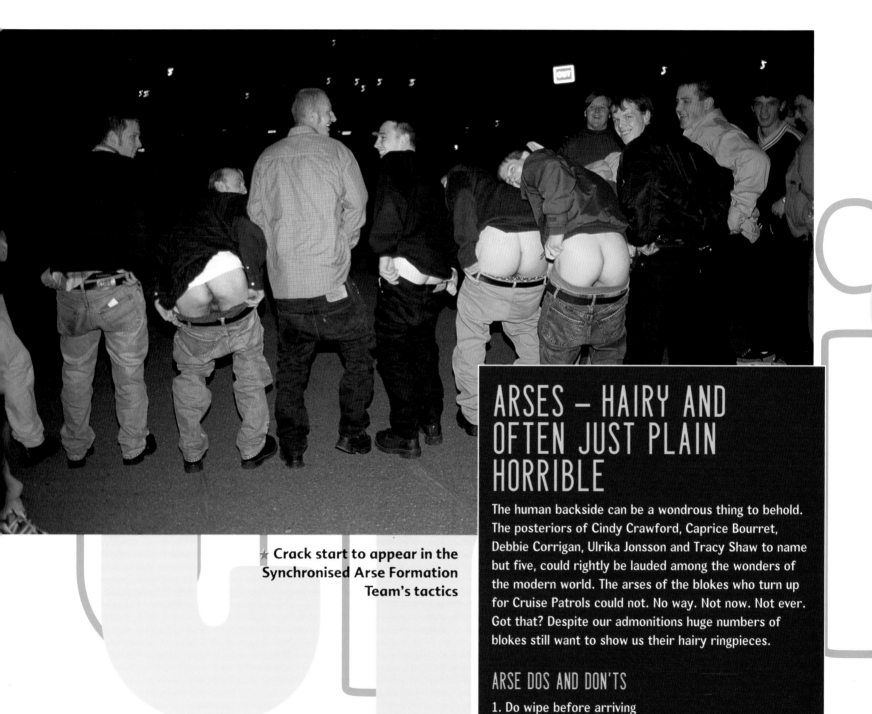

★ **Crack start to appear in the Synchronised Arse Formation Team's tactics**

ARSES – HAIRY AND OFTEN JUST PLAIN HORRIBLE

The human backside can be a wondrous thing to behold. The posteriors of Cindy Crawford, Caprice Bourret, Debbie Corrigan, Ulrika Jonsson and Tracy Shaw to name but five, could rightly be lauded among the wonders of the modern world. The arses of the blokes who turn up for Cruise Patrols could not. No way. Not now. Not ever. Got that? Despite our admonitions huge numbers of blokes still want to show us their hairy ringpieces.

ARSE DOS AND DON'TS

1. Do wipe before arriving

2. Do trim your anal hair

3. Do get your chick to do the same

4. Don't wear Y-fronts

5. Don't have skidmarks

6. Don't shit yourself

★ It is not advisable to borrow your gran's car for a Cruise... 'cos everyone will take the piss out of you.

BLUE MOON: 3 STEPS TO HEAVEN

1. Clean your grindles before leaving the house. Sandblast it if you have to.

2. Adopt the requisite pose, then drop those strides and pants. For maximum effect do both these at the same time.

3. Yank those cheeks apart so all around can check if you followed instruction number 1.

TOTTY – NOT THE SHY SORT

Most cruise totty tend to be fit, have massive mams and be up for it in a big way. This is because they usually turn up shitted in their boyfriend's car and by about 9.30pm are up for anything. Nearly. Our particular faves include showing their knicks, tits or the all-time high – girl-girl action with a similarly-minded female.

A Max Totty Needs

1. Wonderbra or similar chest-enhancing garment

2. Short skirt

3. A good seeing-to

A Max Totty Doesn't Need

1. Much encouragement

2. Much booze

3. Any more perfume

★ A pair of breasts, yesterday.

★ There's always one who just has to show her knickers. Well done, girl.

★ **How to make a hash of modifying your car.**

★ **The designers worked long into the night developing the new Max Power bra.**

HOW TO FUCK UP YOUR ENGINE – THE BURN OUT WAY

You can gain top respect at Cruise Patrols by having twenty blokes sitting on your bonnet before your car disappears in clouds of smoke. If you want to be accorded the title, "Top Man," then keep the burn out going until your brand spanking new A510s burst and the alloys burn down to the hubs and blow up. Of course, having to get Pugh, Pew, Barney McGrew, Cuthbert, Dibble and Grub out to put out the fire is going a tad far but their flashing lights and weird wailing noises always add to the evening's entertainment.

ARSE DOS AND DON'TS

1. Do them often

2. Do them under the eagle eye of the Old Bill with a naked bit of crumpet sticking out of the sunroof

3. Don't attempt one if your clutch is buggered – being laughed at can be a humiliating experience

4. Don't burst the tyres if you are overly fond of your bodykit

5. Don't use your own car

TITS OUT FOR THE LADS

1. Wear an Ultra Bra or a Wonderbra that shows off your cleavage but refuse to reveal those funbags until the crowd is baying for them.

2. Get the punters excited by shaking your tits about.

3. Get yer tits out for the lads – you know you wanted to all along. Unhook your bra and... Yes!

★ **'You on the end, this isn't a bra commercial.'**

★ **'Help! My left hand's caught in a helicopter!'**

HOW TO SCORE (REMEMBER, POINTS MEAN PRIZES)...

★ Group burn outs/tits out/moonies

★ Tits out, or moon in a moving car (but not if you're behind the wheel)

★ Burn outs on holy ground (synagogues, churches, mosques, Highbury, etc.)

★ Mangling as many engine components as possible during burn outs

★ Creating a huge convoy that blocks town centres and important roads...

★ ...forcing the Old Bill to set up roadblocks

★ Putting a Max sticker on a panda car

★ Getting arrested

★ Chundering on an Old Bill car or, for that matter, on Bill himself

...and, most importantly, girl-on-girl action!

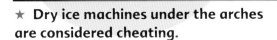

★ **Dry ice machines under the arches are considered cheating.**

★ **Police try to investigate the invasion of bodies from the mysterious planet L.**

THE OLD BILL

No cruise is a complete classic until the Plod turn up in their rowdy vans and arrest a bloke for having tinted windows. What ought to happen, however, is that they should sod off. After all, it can't be much fun being pelted with rotten fruit or taunted with shouts of, 'Who's that twat with the nipple on his hat' and other old family favourites. Still, they hang around wanting to join in the fun too scared to, 'cos of what Sarge will say back at the nick. Jobsworths the lot of them. 'I'm only doing my job,' is their plaintive cry. Fuck off!!! However, to be public spirited it is important that they keep an eye on real crims like us 'cos after all, it's not as if there are any muggers or rapists around, is it?

Things To Say To The Plod

1. 'It's a fair cop guv. You've got me banged to rights'

2. 'I'll come quietly officer'

3. 'Honest, officer, there's nothing to see here'

Things Not To Say To The Plod

1. 'The drugs are up me arse'

2. 'I didn't know I had to get a tax disc every year'

3. 'Who's at home fucking your wife?'

★ **The Old Bill reveal their new undercover team.**

★ 'Tell me, does that tongue stud hurt?... Oooh no, it doesn't, does it?'

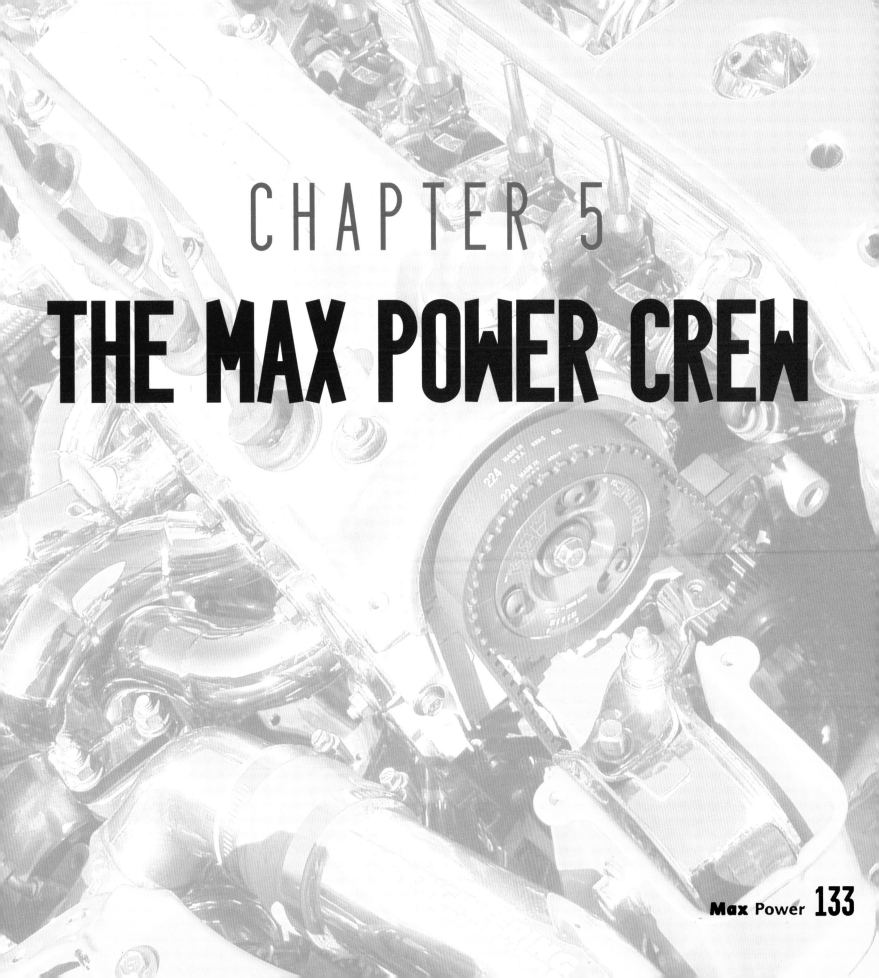

CHAPTER 5
THE MAX POWER CREW

MARTYN MOORE

AGE: 37.

JOBS: Consultant Editor, Associate Editor, Ex-Editor, Editorial Coach.

PREVIOUS JOBS: Photographer, sailor, coffin varnisher.

HOW DID YOU LAND AT PLANET MAX: I was lured by the wicked Editorial Director to teach the writers how to string a sentence together. It's a tough challenge.

CAR (ACTUAL): Rover 216 SLi.

CAR (DREAM): A nice old E-type with wire wheels.

IDEAL PASSENGER: Sophie Raworth (sexy BBC 1 newsreader).

NAUGHTIEST THING YOU'VE DONE IN A CAR: Told the woman I'd just run into the back of to turn left and pull over. I then went straight on.

FAVE NIGHT OUT: Open air classical concert on a warm summer evening, fireworks display, fine wine and then a good stiff shit.

FAVE BAND: The Dagenham Girl Pipers.

FAVE TV SHOW: Seinfeld (unfunny Yank drivel - Hans)

FAVE SEXUAL POSITION: Against the wall.

THE FUTURE: Fuck knows.

RUSTY THE SHERIFF
(It's a long story)

AGE: Mentally 14, physically 54, actually somewhere between the two.

JOB: Production Editor.

PREVIOUS JOBS: Gang leader and robber.

HOW DID YOU LAND AT PLANET MAX: Via a Harrier jump jet.

CAR (ACTUAL): BMW325i.

CAR (DREAM): Big red Ferrari, of course.

IDEAL PASSENGER: Rich and beautiful.

NAUGHTIEST THING YOU'VE DONE IN A CAR: I threw up in my mate's MGB after a huge drinking session on my 21st. I've had a permanent hangover eversince.

FAVE NIGHT OUT: Loadsa Guinness with the lads in a proper boozer like Johnny Byrne's.

FAVE BAND: Tom Petty.

FAVE TV SHOW: Don't do TV.

FAVE SEXUAL POSITION: Leaning on the bar.

THE FUTURE: Computers.

JON 'PROBY' WALSH

AGE: 25.

JOB: ICE Editor.

PREVIOUS JOBS: DJ, Architectural technician, CAD draftsman, hearse driver, professional burglar

HOW DID YOU LAND AT PLANET MAX: A strange mix of misfortune and being kidnapped.

CAR (ACTUAL): Nova (modified).

CAR (DREAM): Fiat Coupé 20v Turbo or Subaru Impreza WRC 22B (a road-going, 2-door, wide-arch WRX replica only available in Japan).

IDEAL PASSENGERS: Sporty Spice and Anna Nicole Smith together, or the three sisters from the Corrs.

NAUGHTIEST THING YOU'VE DONE IN A CAR: 152mph.

FAVE NIGHT OUT: Booze and Playstation, then pub, then club, then curry, then home.

FAVE BANDS: The Corrs, Thomas Lang, anything new.

FAVE TV SHOW: Have I Got News For You?

FAVE SEXUAL POSITION: Hot, wet, noisy.

THE FUTURE: Every day is a winding road...

NIGEL GRIMSHAW

AGE: 32.

JOB: Editor.

PREVIOUS JOB: Journalist on Street Machine, Car Week, Max Power and Revs.

HOW DID YOU LAND AT PLANET MAX: Fate.

CAR (ACTUAL): Renault Clio 16v.

CAR (DREAM): Alfa Romeo SZ.

IDEAL PASSENGER: Melanie Sykes.

NAUGHTIEST THING YOU'VE DONE IN A CAR: 0–60mph in 2.89 seconds (yes, really).

FAVE NIGHT OUT: Long Island Iced Teas and Skunk.

FAVE BAND: Green Day.

FAVE TV SHOW: Star Trek: Voyager.

FAVE SEXUAL POSITION: Anyone I can get.

THE FUTURE: Sex, drink, pleasure.

PAUL BURTON

AGE: 32.

JOB: Designer and certified basket case.

PREVIOUS JOB: Performance Car and much more. Too much to mention.

HOW DID YOU LAND AT PLANET MAX: Made redundo.

CARS (ACTUAL): VW Camper, Escort.

CARS (DREAM): 355, Lancia Hyena, Lambo Miura.

IDEAL PASSENGER: Foxy Brown.

NAUGHTIEST THING YOU'VE DONE IN A CAR: That's very personal and best kept that way.

FAVE NIGHTS OUT: Saturday.

FAVE BANDS: Gomez, Buffalo Springfield, Beck.

FAVE TV SHOW: The Grind.

FAVE SEXUAL POSITION: That's personal.

THE FUTURE: Bar in Mauritius.

MICHELLE COPESTAKE

AGE: 22.

JOB: Office Manager.

PREVIOUS JOBS: Claims handler, secretary.

HOW DID YOU LAND AT PLANET MAX: Flashed my tits. No, seriously I developed large breasts and a brain. An unusual combination.

CAR (ACTUAL): VW Polo 'S' reg.

CAR (DREAM): Merc SLK.

IDEAL PASSENGER: Ewan McGregor.

NAUGHTIEST THING YOU'VE DONE IN A CAR: Can't say.

FAVE NIGHT OUT: Karaoke on a Friday night.

FAVE BAND: The Nolans.

FAVE TV SHOW: South Park.

FAVE SEXUAL POSITION: Doggie-style.

THE FUTURE: Orange.

HANS SEEBERG

AGE: 23.

JOB: Feature writer.

PREVIOUS JOBS: Public school fop, head boy and tennis coach

HOW DID YOU LAND AT PLANET MAX: Employed on the grounds of being able to do a Posh Spice impression.

CAR (ACTUAL): Quad Turbo Uno (Bugatti EB110 engine transplant).

CAR (DREAM): Oct Turbo Uno (Twin Bugatti EB110 engine transplant).

IDEAL PASSENGER: Gail Porter from *Fully Booked.*

NAUGHTIEST THING YOU'VE DONE IN A CAR: Almost followed through in a Skyline.

FAVE NIGHT OUT: GADAB, obviously.

FAVE BAND: Beastie Boys.

FAVE TV SHOW: Wildlife on One, especially when it's about sharks.

FAVE SEXUAL POSITION: Doggie.

THE FUTURE: Becoming the next Norwegian Ambassador.

CARRA TOMS

AGE: 26.

JOB: Graphics designer.

PREVIOUS JOBS: Barmaid, waitress, taxi operator, video shop assistant and various design jobs.

HOW DID YOU LAND AT PLANET MAX: They pleaded with me to take the job.

CAR (ACTUAL): Escort Ghia.

CAR (DREAM): Something electric or Puma.

IDEAL PASSENGER: Brad Pitt or Will Smith.

NAUGHTIEST THING YOU'VE DONE IN A CAR: Apart from the obvious, shooting people out the car window with a toy uzi. The police eventually confiscated the gun, although I can't really remember that bit. I was completely stoned.

FAVE NIGHT OUT: Getting high and camping on the beach underneath the stars.

FAVE BAND: Rattle Plaster.

FAVE TV SHOW: Star Trek.

FAVE SEXUAL POSITION: Standing up in the shower.

THE FUTURE: To go to the moon.

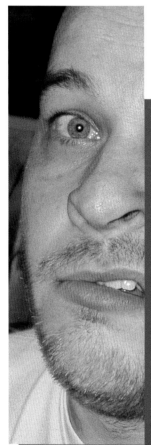

DAMON COGMAN

AGE: 14.

JOB: Chief colouring-in person.

PREVIOUS JOB: Lettuce cutter in the Fens.

HOW DID YOU LAND AT PLANET MAX: On my arse.

CARS (ACTUAL): I've got loads, because I'm wadded.

CAR (DREAM): 'General Lee' from *The Dukes of Hazzard*.

IDEAL PASSENGERS: Anna Nicole Smith getting it on with Linsey Dawn McKenzie or Daisy Duke from The Dukes of Hazzard.

NAUGHTIEST THING YOU'VE DONE IN A CAR: Crashing a £30,000 Westfield V8 100 yards from the office.

FAVE NIGHT OUT: I'm agoraphobic so I don't go out much.

FAVE BAND: Drum and Bangra with a hint of Chutney.

FAVE TV SHOW: South Park.

FAVE SEXUAL POSITION: Number 367.

THE FUTURE: Is a wonder to behold.

'ARTHUR' JOHN SOOTHERAN

AGE: 31 going on 18.

JOB: Deputy Editor.

PREVIOUS JOBS: Quality controller in a frozen chip factory (really!), security guard at Sydney stock exchange, freelance writer for hardcore pornography magazines, freelance photographer (for Practical Photography).

HOW DID YOU LAND AT PLANET MAX: Did two 'Crown to Towns' – 17-pub crawl – with the Max team.

CAR (ACTUAL): Perfect Pug.

CAR (DREAM): Ferrari 550 Maranello.

IDEAL PASSENGER: Nicole Kidman (sorry Tom!) or Melanie Sykes.

NAUGHTIEST THING YOU'VE DONE IN A CAR: She was ten years older than me and only wearing a fur coat.

FAVE NIGHT OUT: GADAB, obviously.

FAVE BAND: Nick Cave.

FAVE TV SHOW: Married...with children.

FAVE SEXUAL POSITION: I'm fond of 69!

THE FUTURE: Extending my already vast pornography collection.

GEZ JONES

AGE: 28.

JOB: Consumer Editor.

PREVIOUS JOBS: Butcher, carpenter, boat-builder, mountain-bike racer and freelance journalist before finally joining Max Power.

HOW DID YOU LAND AT PLANET MAX: On my feet.

CAR (ACTUAL): Alfa Romeo 75 3.0 V6.

CAR (DREAM): Porsche 959 twin turbo.

IDEAL PASSENGER: Any loose woman.

NAUGHTIEST THING YOU'VE DONE IN A CAR: I once refused to eat my vegetables in an Audi Coupé.

FAVE NIGHT OUT: GADAB, obviously.

FAVE BAND: Rubber.

FAVE TV SHOW: Any porn or The Simpsons.

FAVE SEXUAL POSITION: From behind.

THE FUTURE: I hope so.

NICK TROTT

AGE: 24.

JOB: Features writer.

PREVIOUS JOBS: Barman, freelance writer for Bliss.

HOW DID YOU LAND AT PLANET MAX: At the interview I said it was crap and claimed I could make it better.

CAR (ACTUAL): Citroën AX GT.

CAR (DREAM): Porsche 917.

IDEAL PASSENGER: Yasmine Bleeth.

NAUGHTIEST THING YOU'VE DONE IN A CAR: You name it.

FAVE NIGHT OUT: Booze, bonfire, barbecue, birds and a beach in Cornwall – perfect.

FAVE BAND: Monster Magnet.

FAVE TV SHOW: The Prisoner.

FAVE SEXUAL POSITION: Mongolian Cluster Fuck!

THE FUTURE: is ginger.

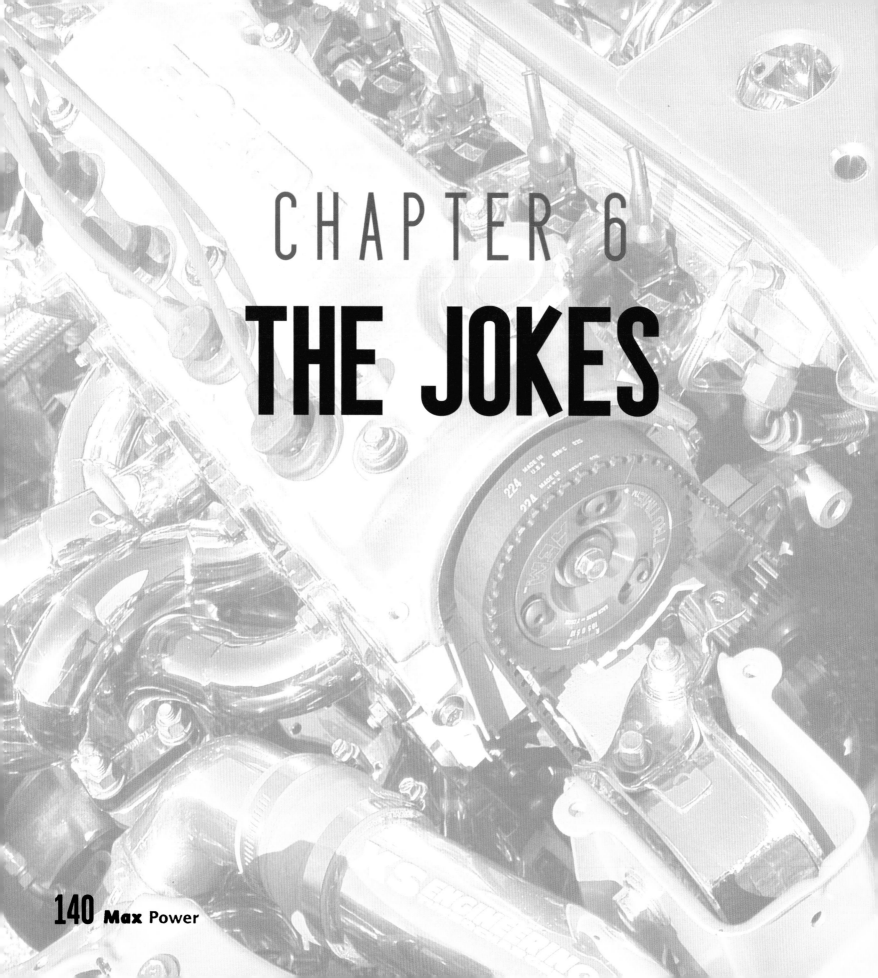

CHAPTER 6
THE JOKES

A BLOKE is in a nightclub and tries to chat up this bird but with no success. Finally, he takes a small box from his pocket. In it is a little frog. 'This frog can do amazing tricks,' boasts the man. 'Such as?' asks the bird. 'He eats pussy. Come back to my place and I'll prove it.' Intrigued, the girl goes back with him, strips off and lays on the bed. The bloke puts the frog between her legs but it just sits there doing nothing. The bird says, 'Well?' The man sighs, picks up the frog and says, 'Right this is the last time I'm going to show you.'

SINCE THEY were wed Jane has nagged her husband about how many women he has slept with. 'If I told you, you'd get angry,' he says. 'No, I won't. I promise. Come on, tell me.' 'Okay, if you're sure.' 'I'm sure.' 'Okay, here goes. One...two...three...you... five...six...'

THIS WOMAN complains to her friend that her husband has lost interest in her and prefers a night out with the boys to a night in with her. Her friend advises her to make more of an effort – cook him a fab meal, send him to the pub and then wear her sexiest undies for when he returns. She follows the advice and when he returns she is dressed in a sexy basque. When he sees her lying decorously on the bed, he tells her to stand up and strip off. Then he tells her to perform a handstand against the bedroom mirror and open her legs. She does this and he puts his head between her legs and looks in the mirror. She feels excited, then he says, 'No, perhaps the boys are right. A beard wouldn't suit me.'

AN ARMLESS, legless man is sunbathing on the beach when these three gorgeous women approach him. The first one says, 'Have you ever been hugged?' He says 'no', so she hugs him. The second one says, 'Have you ever been kissed?' He says 'no', so she kisses him. The third one says, 'Have you ever been fucked?' His eyes light up and he says 'no'. She says, 'Well you are now, the tide's coming in.'

WHAT'S THE difference between BSE and PMT? One's a mad cow disease, the other's a farming problem.

ALAN IS walking past his parents' open bedroom door on his way to the bog when he sees his father giving his mother one. In the morning he asks his father, 'Daddy, why were you doing that to mummy last night?' 'Because mummy wants a baby.' The next night on his way to the bog he sees his mother giving his father a blowjob. In the morning he asks his father, 'Daddy, why was Mummy doing that to you last night?' 'Because mummy wants a BMW.'

"HERE IS a newsflash. A burglary was committed last night at Maine Road, home of Manchester City FC and the entire contents of the trophy room were stolen. Police are looking for a man with a pale blue carpet."

TWO NUNS are driving along a country road when this naked bloke jumps in front of the car and begins dancing lewdly. 'What shall I do, Sister?' asks the first. 'Show him your cross,' says the second. So she winds down the window and shouts, 'Oi mate, get the fuck out of the road!'

A DRUNK wanders into a church and stumbles towards the confessional watched by the priest. The drunk enters the confessional and sits down. Noises are heard by the priest who coughs. No reply so he coughs again. Still no reply so the priest knocks on the wall. 'Itsh no good knocking, mate,' says the drunk. 'There'sh no loo paper in thish one either.'

THIS WOMAN is lying in the road after being run over. The driver gets out and asks if she is okay. 'You're a blur so my sight must be affected,' she says. Concerned, he decides to test her eyesight. 'How many fingers have I got up?' he asks. 'Oh fuck,' says the woman, 'I must be paralysed from the waist down as well.'

A BREED of rare gorilla is about to die out, as there are only a few left and the only one in captivity is in a zoo. Time is running out and her biological clock is ticking. The scientists discover a report that says that now man can mate with gorilla. But who would fuck a gorilla? Who better than Mick, her keeper for the past 22 years. They call him and suggest the idea to him. 'We know she's really close to you.' 'Yep, she's like a close friend.' 'We need someone to mate with her and propagate the species. It needs to be done quickly and we think you are the perfect guy to do this.' Mick thinks for a while then says no. The scientists says, 'It's a £1000 deal but must be cloaked in secrecy. It will help the species to survive and it will be all thanks to you.' Mick asks for a day to think it over. The next day he goes to see the scientists and says, 'I'll do it but there are three conditions.' 'What are they?' ask the scientists. 'Firstly, no kissing on the lips. Secondly,

any children born must be raised as Roman Catholics.' 'That's all fine,' says the scientists. 'What's the third condition?' 'Well, you'll have to give me a week to get the £1000 together.'

HOW DO you know when it's time to clean the house and do the washing up? Look inside your pants. If you have a dick, it's not time.

A COUPLE are running short of money so they agree the wife should go on the game. Her husband picks her up after her first night of streetwalking. 'How much did you make?' he asks. '£18.50,' she says. 'That's not bad, who gave you 50p?' 'They all did.'

A BIG-TITTED, attractive girl gets on a bus and sees this fanciable bloke sitting opposite her. She smiles at him but gets no reaction so she undoes the top buttons on her blouse to show him her cleavage. Still no reaction so she hoists up her skirt to show her stocking tops. She still gets no reaction from him so she yanks off her knickers, leaps onto the seat and sits on his face. He smiles and says, 'I may be blind but I know that smell anywhere. It's Grimsby, my stop.'

BERT AND Doris have been together for 60 years and live in a sheltered accommodation. One day Bert comes into their room and tells Doris he's leaving her for their next door neighbour Mildrid. 'But why?' 'She gives me oral sex.' 'But Bert I give you oral sex.' 'I know – but you haven't got Parkinson's Disease.'

VIRGINIA HAS led a very sheltered life and is still a virgin on her wedding night. So in order to reassure her, Mark her husband allows her mother to come on honeymoon with them. The mother waits in another room while the happy couple get down to it. As Mark undresses Virginia is horrified to see his hairy chest. She rushes in to see her mother, 'Mum, Mark has got a hairy chest.' 'Go back to your

SIX LIES MEN TELL WOMEN AND WHAT THEY REALLY MEAN

1. HE SAYS "Yes, I do have a girlfriend, but it's an open relationship."
HE MEANS "I'm engaged but she's away for a week."

2. HE SAYS "I love you."
HE MEANS "I fancy you."

3. HE SAYS "You are stunningly gorgeous."
HE MEANS "I'm desperate for a shag."

4. HE SAYS "I've never done this before."
HE MEANS "That's what I said last Friday and it worked then."

5. HE SAYS "I live too far away, why don't we go back to your place?"
HE MEANS "My girlfriend's due over in the morning."

6. HE SAYS "You aren't fat."
HE MEANS "You are fat but I'm desperate for a shag."

room and don't worry darling, all good men have hairy chests.' Reassured Virginia goes back to the room. Mark takes his trousers off and Virginia is horrified to see his hairy legs. She rushes in to see her mother, 'Mum, Mark has got hairy legs.' 'Don't worry darling, all good men have hairy legs. Go back to your room.' Reassured Virginia goes back to the room. When Mark takes his socks off he has no toes on his left foot. Virginia rushes in to see her mother, 'Mum, Mark has got a foot and a half.' The mother gets up, 'You sit down there, darling. This is a job for your mother.'

WHAT'S THE connection between a fat woman and a moped? They're both great rides until your mates see you on one.

TWO DWARVES win a million on the lottery so they decide to book two hookers and take them to a hotel. So they get to their rooms but the first dwarf can't get it up and all he hears from the other room is 'One, two, three, huh!' By the morning he still hasn't been able to get it up. The second dwarf asks, 'How was it?' 'Awful,' said the first. 'I couldn't get an erection. How was your night?' 'Even worse, I couldn't even get onto the bed.'

WHEN HE is delivering the daily milk a milkman finds a note asking for 50 pints. He knocks on the door and a sexy blonde woman answers. 'Is this a mistake,' asks Milko. 'No, I saw an article which said bathing in milk was good for your complexion,' says the woman. 'Oh okay. Do you want it pasteurised?' 'No, up to my tits will be fine.'

THANKS FOR THE PHOTOS:

FLY:	Astra, RS Turbo, CRX, Skyline, Pug 306, Citroen AX, Golf, Lambo Diablo
KENNY P:	BMW Compact, Escort 2000, BMW323i, BMW Z3, BMW325i, Cavalier, Calibra
GUS GREGORY:	Nissan, Ka
JOHN STODDART:	Kaja
JULIAN CALVERLY:	Yasmin, Claire
DUNCAN LOUGHREY:	Aleeka and Debbie Turpin

The author and publishers have made every reasonable effort to contact all copyright holders. Any errors that may have occurred are inadvertent and anyone who for any reason has not been contacted is invited to write to the publishers so that a full acknowledgement may be made in subsequent editions of this work.

ACKNOWLEDGEMENTS

My first debt of gratitude goes to the people without whom this book really would not exist – the staff of Max Power, past and present, especially Nigel Grimshaw, Jon Walsh, Michelle Copestake and Bill Thomas who performed above and beyond the call of duty.

I'm also grateful to my friend Andy Lander for helping to 'max' my own car; and to Anne-Marie Morris, who burned out her car on a Cruise Patrol, for her encouragement.

This is my first collaboration (hopefully of many) with André Deutsch where Hannah MacDonald proved herself an indomitable force in getting things done and an excellent editor to boot. What more could any writer ask for?

Thanks, as always, to the pulchritudinous Sharon Hall.

My agent, Chelsey Fox of the Fox & Howard Literary Agency, is to be recommended to any author seeking representation. Her wise and generous counsel is always well-heeded.

If you have any comments on the cars/ICE/totty featured in this book, you can e-mail me at paul@uk.com

Finally, this book is dedicated to my father as a very small token for all that I owe him.

Paul Donnelley, July 1998